Dr Nona J

Embracing Change

Painlessly

Maximising The Mind - Engaging God's Word

(Mind Workout Gym Series - Vol 1)

Nukan Publications

"A man is literally what he thinks, his character being the complete sum of all his thoughts.
As a plant springs from and could not be without the seed, so every act of a man springs from the hidden seeds of thought, and could not have appeared without them. This applies equally to those acts "spontaneous" and "unpremeditated" as to those which are deliberately excused."

- James Allen (*As A Man Thinketh*)

"We are what we repeatedly do. Excellence then is not an act, but a habit."

- Aristotle

"Your power to choose is the secret to great attitudes."

- Chuck R Swindoll

It's Your Choice To Enjoy Life;
No Matter What.

Embracing Change Painlessly
(Maximising the Mind - Engaging God's Word)
By Dr Nona Joyce Edeki

Copyright © 2021 Dr Nona Joyce Edeki

ISBN-13: 978-1545048610
ISBN-10: 1545048614

Publisher: Nukan Publications

Basildon, Essex, UK

First Printed: 2021

Cover Design: Design2Impact.co.uk

Dedication

To the Lord God Almighty, who has been my faithful and dependable Refuge over the years.

Praise the Lord!

To my wonderful and amiable sons, Dr(s) Ohiomoje, Ohilebo and Joshua - who are now men. Glory be to God! They have taught me many things over the years and more importantly, they are my #1 fans.

"The Lord has done this, and it is marvelous in our eyes"
Psalm 118:23

Acknowledgement

Firstly, I thank God Almighty that I have the privilege of knowing Him. My relationship with God is one, which I can completely rely on - no matter what! Through the valley and mountain-top experiences of life, I have come to know beyond doubt and understand that God is not only dependable but also reliable! I have come to enjoy this reliability and constancy of His love that now I know beyond all reasoning hence I say 'in the mathematical arithmetic of my life; God, His Word and The Holy Spirit - The THREE IN ONE GOD is and remains the CONSTANT in the equation of my life. He is totally immersed with the fabric of who I am, today and forever. He will be, always.

I wish to acknowledge my three wonderful sons who have been a source of inspiration; and from whom I have learnt so much about myself. Their testimonies challenge me to the holy calling. Today, I can say that I am highly optimistic and enthused to embrace the changes in each day despite all the challenges I have been through. Amen.

Finally, I want to thank my parents, who nurtured me to embrace life holistically.

I cannot forget to thank all my audiences around the world as well as friends and extended family without whose support, this work would not be possible. I appreciate you all and thank you for the opportunity to serve God by sharing His love through His word.

My prayer is that we all will come to see the

importance of the Word of God in scriptures and embrace change in obedience, until God's Word is craftily woven and etched in all our hearts and minds.

"Thy Word is a lamp unto my feet and a light unto my path" - Psalm 119:105 (KJV)

Endorsement by
Reverend (Mrs) Julie Akhimien

Embracing Change Painlessly using God's Word is more than just a book, it is the gateway to limitless opportunities to achieving purpose in life by Divine Enablement.

It is indeed a Masters' degree on how to obtain the mindset that is courageous in a world filled with uncertainties and chaos.

In it, Dr. Joyce Edeki examines the core aspects of God's creation: The human mind and offers practical solutions on how to bring about a desired change using The Word of God.

There are so many levels to the mind that makes one eager to learn more and more as you go through the Divinely-inspired pages of this book.

Embracing Change Painlessly is applicable to all and sundry; the old and the young, male or female, irrespective of race or colour, social status or geographical location because the God who owns us all is intentionally involved in each evolving chapter of the book as everyday issues of life are addressed, precept upon precept, line upon line; you will find yourself unwilling to let this book out of sight!

It is a book to be read and referred to time and time again because it shows how to apply God's Word to bring about that change that is most necessary; following the principles of the God who cannot CHANGE but can change things, times and seasons.

The Word works and that is why this book unravels the mystery which many individuals may struggle with in life.

The Author certainly had a Divine Inspiration from the Throne of Grace as shown in the way she has carefully and painstakingly examined the subject matter. Simple but profound ways in applying God's Word as you go through the change process.

You made the best decision ever choosing a book so inspiring. Congratulations.

Rev. (Mrs) Julie Akhimien.
National President
Christian Women Fellowship Int'l (CWFI)

Foreword

At a time when the world is constantly changing and when we are all being encouraged to embrace change, not just at an individual level but also as citizens of the earth; this book could not have come at a better time.

As you journey with Dr Edeki in this book, you will notice her assertiveness about her faith and self-identity. She explains to her readers how faith helps us to define who we are and gives us strength to navigate changes that life throws at us.

The book taps into Joyce's many years of experience as a psychiatrist, including discussions about the commonest drug of addiction in our society, the theory behind non-pharmacological therapies and the bio-psychosocial model of diseases and recovery. She also did not fail to highlight her signature therapy of Mind Workout Gym (MWG).

As asserted by Joyce in this book, "change is the only constant factor" and when life throws you lemons, try to make lemonade with them and you may just be amazed how the Spirit of God will breathe on your lemonade and turn it to the "wine of life".

Whilst no one can promise what tomorrow brings, we however, know of a God who owns tomorrow. He is the God of ages past and the hopes of years to come. I will thus like to thank Joyce for all she does for the body of

Christ and also for using her own life experiences to illustrate how we can be EMBRACING CHANGE.

The Revd. Dr. S. Osunsanmi
Missionary Priest (Church of Nigeria)
Associate Priest (Church of England)
Child and Adolescent Psychiatrist

Table of Contents

Preface

There is no living being who has not met situations that warrant some form of change or another in its entire life. Life itself is one huge continuum of change! I have had to engage these changes on many occasions even when I did not think I was ready. Embracing change is all about living, adaptability, flexibility, open mindedness and being willing to explore even the unknown - areas outside our comfort zones.

The very idea of 'being' is all about EMBRACING. My wish has always been to be in a position to share some lessons of life in a book; however, the timing never seemed to be right – until now. In my fifty odd years on earth, life has brought along challenges; my willingness to face those challenges head-on has meant that I have had to embrace significant change in my being. I share some of very key lessons in this book. Writing this book called for a change in my normal daily routine and completing it is indeed an accomplished personal goal.

This book has been in the pipeline for years and sometimes I wondered if it will ever get to the publishers. This is because I have been procrastinating! Yes, I have been doing just that. The thief of time, it is called, procrastination. I thank God that He helped me overcome that hurdle. The moment is here and is now. God always has the perfect timing.

Keep faith and hope alive.

Introduction

Over the five decades I have lived on this earth, I have come to know that some things are true beyond reason such as the existence of God; the efficacy of the Word of God and being obedient to the Word. I have made small but impactful changes in my life that has enabled me see progress in many areas of my life. I always wished I could get conscripted into the Army. Do you know why this was, because I so wanted to be able consistently demonstrate discipline in every area of my life.

Immediately I left University, I got married and started making children. My desire to live a consistently disciplined and more productive life surely became one to put on the shelf. However, I prayed, prayed some more and read self-help books to get quick strategies, all to no avail. I only started to see a glimpse of my desire when I made the choice to obey God's Word one step at a time. I chose to just act on the Word. Success and happiness in life is a process which happens in baby steps. Every aspect of my life has gradually unfolded in a more disciplined way ever since.

I have also come to know that living a life outside of God and His word is synonymous with heading to the frontlines of war without necessary defense gear.

You may ask me how did I come to such a conclusions or even be so sure of God's existence; in other words, how do I know God exists?

As much as I know the answer to this lies within my own transformative experiences, real time encounters with God's word further strengthens not only my affirmation in the existence of God, but also the legitimacy of my relationship with Him. I know that I know beyond any reasonable doubt that God is real and that this relationship I have with Him is as real as it can be. I communicate with HIM daily in prayer and in my thoughts; yes, in my thoughts! I enjoy and hear His voice from His Word contained in the Bible as well as from inner witness in my spirit. I have come to find joy and real sense of my life's plan and purposes. This (God and me) relationship has sated the deep spiritual needs as well as satisfied the deeper inner sense of connection with my Maker; the result of which is a transformed life of peace and enjoyment no matter what comes my way. This desire and longing for the divine, I believe, is innate in every cognitive and living being.

God has created us, humans, to have a deep yearning for that which is beyond the realms of the physical, and this yearn ultimately is satisfied only in and with Him. A vacuum creates a sense of 'void and emptiness', which can only be satisfied by Him and His love alone.

In addition, the evidence of God's existence not only lies in the miraculous workings in the lives of men and women across the world, but in the beauty of nature that surrounds us; and most of all, in the infallible evidence in scriptures as contained in the BIBLE.

I could not talk about embracing change without describing the powerful change that is taking place in my life every day because I made a conscious attempt to know

God. I have deliberately made that choice, to know and experience God for myself; there is a depth of conviction that arises from experience, and that is the power of knowing that you know.

I know that God IS. Period!

I fear what my life would have been without God. Not even to mention where I probably could have been now.

Knowing God is the beginning of wisdom and the secret of enjoying life here on earth. It is the most rewarding, constant and dependable relationship I have ever known. I relate with God as a father, husband and as my closest friend. I feel lost and completely disconnected when, for any reason, I do not feel His closeness and presence on a daily basis. There is no enjoyment in this life or calming peace (described as that which passes all human understanding) that can be compared to being with and enjoying God's presence daily. Cultivating closeness to God and a habit of enjoying fellowship with Him is the greatest and most peaceful state any human can desire. The peace, contentment, joy and satisfaction one experiences is indescribable. In His presence, there is fullness of joy and at His right hand are pleasures forevermore. We, as humans, can experience the most transformational change consciously and unconsciously, bodily, spiritually, emotionally and intellectually.

Every form and level of change is possible depending on our belief/value systems and our choices especially how we receive the seed of God's Word, as well as how we perceive God and the world around us. I will be making references to the Word of God frequently in this book because as far as I know, The Word of God as contained in the BIBLE; (BIBLE acronym: Basic Instructions Before Leaving Earth) holds the key to the transformation and change referred to throughout in this book.

I am not a fan of the big bang theory; neither am I, of the Darwin's theories. Firstly, these theories were postulated by mere mortal men. Men's ideas postulated as scientific evidence. Secondly, I chose to believe the biblical account of creation, because therein is reason and logic that my little mind can make out sense of. There is a loving God; Who after making the heavens and the earth, He decided to make man (you and I) in His image and likeness, the Bible tells me. It does not matter much what you think is behind the creation, what is key is the fact that I choose to believe that I was created by a great big and loving God who is good, compassionate and full of ALL wisdom. My ancestry is in God's lineage and not in apes and other concepts.

We, humans, are the handiwork of God. Just ponder on this. How did it happen that the making of you might have survived the natural selection process before you were born; or even how the egg and sperm from your parents, united amongst the many others to form you in your mothers' womb? Just how did you make it despite all the odds? This is why I often say that it is a privilege to be me, occupying some space on this planet. I am unique, I have an identity, a purpose and a destiny. That I am still standing here means that I've got work to do!

I have written this book from a Christian perspective and even if you are not a Christian, I am confident that with an open mind, you just may find some real insight and benefit in the views expressed. Happy reading!

Chapter 1

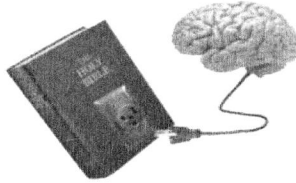

The God Who Changes Us

The Bible describes the most incredible of stories ever told at the beginning of existence. I chose to believe the account in the Bible, which suggests God created man in His likeness and image. I am made in God's own image and likeness (Genesis 1:26) and sure enough, that really makes me feel very special indeed.

At the same time God made this proclamation, He stated our form – to be in His likeness and His image; and an aspect of our purpose here on earth – to have dominion over all the earth and all that He had created. Wow! As if that was not enough, in verse 28 of the same chapter of Genesis, God declared that we should be fruitful and multiply, and replenish the earth, and subdue it and have dominion over every living thing. Wow! Wow!! This is the God I introduce to you today. He speaks and things come to pass just as He has stated.

But God made you and I in His image (a visual representation of something) and likeness (the fact or quality of being alike; a resemblance)

So you and I should have the fact or quality of being alike; and with a resemblance to God. Ponder on this for a moment.

Genesis 1:1-2 describes events and exact state of the earth at creation. (The earth was without form and void, and darkness was upon the face of the deep!). God is excellent and all knowing! He decided to create the Universe and all that we know, out of the nothingness that existed. From the story of the creation account in Genesis, one can extrapolate that God was not pleased with the state of the earth as v2 says: "The earth was without form and void, and darkness was upon the face of the very great deep". Humanly speaking, I would have thought the earth to be very, very boring to behold; let alone for any existence. Presumably, God had a far better idea or indeed held an image of what He desired in Himself. In other words, He had imagined exactly what He desired the earth to look like, feel like, smell and be like; and for a change state to happen, He had to do something to bring what was well-formed in His imagination into the realms of reality – (our kind of reality), as I understand it. He was desirous of change instead of the status quo of the earth.

And what did God do about the situation? God spoke His imagined inner thoughts into existence and then His Spirit, The Holy Spirit, (who is alive today and is the living third Person of the Trinity) moved upon the face of the waters to activate that spoken Word of God into Gods intention.

Behold, creation came into being. What an incredible God!

After God had created time to bind all that He was to create, He spoke day and night into existence right at the very beginning. The Bible records that God frequently reviewed and appraised every stage of His work during the creation process. He looked at the reality that came out of His imagination and thought and saw that it was good, and very good indeed! Genesis 1:21, 25 & 31 record the many times God looked upon what He had created and the satisfaction He must have had, that all was in perfect order and in accordance with the imagined state. At the very end of the beautiful work done, God decided that He will make man after His image and likeness, (Genesis 1:26-27). God had a definite plan with you and I as part of that right before the very beginning. He chose to make man in His own image. The purpose of enjoying fellowship with Him.

Mindworkout Exercise:

Now we know we are made in Gods image and likeness, Practice reminding yourself twice daily, preferable first thing in the morning and last thing at night, say it out to yourself "I am made in Gods image and likeness, I have Gods ability to create in me, I am loved by God"

Think about times you have imagined something; how and when did this become your reality? Did you speak it into existence like your maker?

To experience this quality of God, your words need to

align with what you hold in your mind, your imagination, thoughts, ideas and visions.

To think that God had me in mind while He created this earth and all that we see, makes me feel special! He then decided to make me in His very own nature and likeness. That is just beyond what my little mind can comprehend, but it is true. That is the account recorded in the Bible. The Bible is and remains the number one bestseller across the world. What does that tell you? The content is worth a treasure, at least worth reading once a year and worth applying to our daily lives.

The interesting bit is that its content remains as relevant today as it was 2000 years ago. The heavens and the earth will pass away, not a jot of the Bible's content will pass away.

The Word of God remains eternal and forever constant! What an incredible manual for every created human on earth, to study and live by. This is one of the reasons why I believe that the Bible is the gold standard manual for navigating through this life.

Without the Owner's manual, the consumer is unable to assemble and put together if and when broken an invention, so it is with us human beings and the Word of God.

So How Much Like God Are We?

By deduction, as God exists in three persons, so the human exists also. Humans exist in three entities - spirit, soul and body. The existence of God in three beings alludes to the triune nature of God. The Bible tells us that

God exists in three persons - God the Father, God the Holy Spirit and God the Son - Jesus Christ - The written Word of God personified (who was in the flesh and had a body, walked upon the face of this earth over 2000 years ago). God exists simultaneously as THREE persons in ONE! It is incredible and we as humans can relate to this because we also exist in three entities. Did you know that you have a spirit, a soul which both reside within the outer flesh and blood we see called the body?

I cannot claim to know how this is but I have accepted and believed this fact as well as experienced the THREE PERSONS IN ONE GOD at varied stages of my life. I also accept the wordings in this scripture Deuteronomy 29:29 (KJV) which says: "The secret things belong unto the Lord our God: but those things which are revealed belong unto us and to our children forever, that we may do all the words of this law".

At creation, the scriptures allude to this in Genesis 1:26, God said, "Let us make man in our image, after our likeness." Note the words in bold print **"our"**. If God was alone and not with other persons, He would not repeatedly state the word 'our'. Earlier in the same chapter, there was the mention of the presence of the Holy Spirit hovering over the waters. You may be wondering where Jesus was at creation, right? Apostle John, the son of Zebedee and brother of James, often described as Jesus best friend, records in one of the New Testament account he authored, John 1.1, "In the beginning was the Word, and the Word was with God, and the Word was God". And in the same chapter and in verse 14, Apostle John writes again, "And the Word became flesh and dwelt among us, and we beheld His glory, the glory as of the only begotten of the Father, full of grace and truth. I quote Dr. David Jeremiah, a renowned American Bible teacher "John's Gospel comes with its own clear statement of purpose. At the conclusion of his account, the apostle writes: But these are written that you may believe that Jesus is the Christ, the Son of God, and that believing you may have life in His name" (John 20:31). Johns eye witness testimonies can serve both to stimulate new belief and substantiate existing belief. In either case, John wrote to encourage faith in the only Son of God, that all who believe in Him might have everlasting life (John 3:16). In all that John wrote, his goal was to portray Christ as the divine Son of God clothed in human flesh, having come to save all who believe in Him (John 1:14; 3:16 and 20:30,31).

Each Person in the Trinity has specific roles to play in creation and also in our relationship and walk with God. Our spirits are the aspects which directly link up with The Holy Spirit, our souls can be influenced and transformed by the Holy Spirit, the Word and by our fleshly dictates. Our body which is in direct contact with the earth and our environment as we know it, houses them all – spirit, soul and body. So each aspect of the human being has specific roles to play. While this is not a theological text, suffice to mention that God exists as three distinct Persons, each Person of the Trinity is fully God and can function as separate entity; yet there is One God. It is a mystery indeed!

If we are God's creation supposing that we believe this to be true, then it means that we are like Him in every way; and that we are wired to have a rich imagination just like God. This imagination is one that we can achieve in reality (we need to develop this!); what we desire and have imagined we can also birth into reality. We can seek change and speak the change into existence in our everyday lives. Like Father, like son; remember that we were created in God's image and likeness.

From what we have been trying to describe, we have God's creative ability within us. We need to embrace and believe this concept first before we begin to explore how it can come about. We need to appreciate our dependency on God's ability to help our minds embrace this revelation and accept it that we have been living far below the level of operation that God had intended for us as "creative beings".

What we believe is important and who we believe is equally crucial to making our imagined dreams come to reality.

Knowing the Creator

God is. Period! The moment we begin to question the existence of God, we are on the slippery slope and on a path to destruction. God is the 'I AM THAT I AM'. He is the all-knowing One Who is able to do what He only is able to do. He judges you by the intentions behind the thoughts or the actions we display. Although God's nature is that of goodness and abundant mercy towards us all, One who knows our frailty; He is also described as a Consuming Fire! He judges us by what intents and thoughts run behind the scenes. We must be care ful of the thoughts we entertain and cultivate. According to the scripture in Proverbs 23:7 "For as a man thinks in his heart so is he" You think in secret and it comes to pass. Your thoughts are powerful and yet naked before your maker. Your character is the sum of all your thoughts!

You need to learn how to embrace the virtues of God in your thoughts, and this can only be by the study of God's Word; thereby knowing this awesome God!

Knowing the Creator, gives us the power to become the sons of God. This does not just mean to know about God, but to truly know Him for yourself, within the context of a loving relationship (John 1:12). No one can know another in a meaningful way without truly loving the other. Jesus, teaching his disciples that we all must obey God's commandments, concluding that loving God with all our hearts, all our soul and strengths comes first; and the second law, which was again rooted in love, is that we should love our neighbours as ourselves.

Earlier we read a scripture in John 10:10 where Jesus described that He had come that we may have life and have this life more abundantly. However, for anyone to qualify for this enjoyment, one must seek to know and sincerely love God as Father and He has to know you as one of His children. You and I have to believe that He is and that He is a rewarder of anyone who diligently seeks to know Him (Hebrews 11:6)

A man can become by discovery, soul searching, and intense seeking from the makers manual, can he become all that he is created to be? Good thoughts rooted deep in the Word of God brings forth good fruit; and the soul attracts that which it secretly harbors. Bad thoughts bring forth bad fruit.

<u>**MindWorkout Gym Exercise:**</u>

Do you believe (deep within the depths of your being) in

God and in His word? Accepting Gods Word as true as it is; is fundamental.

You always get and have in your life what you believe for and speak out.

As many as believe in their hearts on the Name of Jesus Christ and confess that He is Lord, will gain salvation (Romans 10:9-10). To such a person, God reveals Himself and His nature as embodied in His Names! God, as Jehovah Shalom, He becomes peace to your anxious states of restlessness. God, as Jehovah Macseh/Misgab, He becomes a safety tower to those who seek refuge in Him. God, as Jehovah Rapha, He is a healer to those who have infirmities/ailment in their bodies – spirit, soul and body.

Growing and maturing in God comes from a life of obedience to Gods Word; which ultimately equates to spiritual maturity. Seeking to understand the very person of God and allowing His word to impart, transform and change our lives is all that it means to live with meaning and purpose. Living in God's will is knowing what that purpose is through His Word and being fruitful in that purpose. No one can know God without having a loving relationship with Him in the first instance. It is only in the place of a loving relationship that we get close enough to know what is in the mind of the other person. It is the same with God. Knowing about God is not enough, you must know Him for yourself through His Word; habitually studying the Word of God to know and to apply this knowledge in everyday living. This helps us walk in His will for us as individuals.

The first point in knowing God is surrendering the

control of your life to Him. How do you do this? You may wish to join in this simple prayer from the heart along these lines:

> "O God, I come to You as I am, a sinner. I believe in my heart and confess with my mouth that Your Son, Jesus Christ, died for my sins; and He rose from the dead that I may have eternal life.

> Father, please forgive me of all my sins and accept me as Your child as I surrender all control of my life to You.

> Gracious Father, I ask for the gift of the Holy Spirit, my Enabler and Helper, who will help me live this new life in Jesus Name I have prayed, Amen.

> I thank You for all You have done for me. I am grateful for this new birth into Your family; I am now born again."

The angelic Host are rejoicing and jubilating that you made this decision to make Jesus Christ, the Lord of Your life! Congratulations.

This prayer goes in line with what the Bible says in John 3:16-18 (AMP) - *For God so [greatly] loved and dearly prized the world, that He [even] gave His [One and] only begotten Son, so that whoever believes and trusts in Him [as Saviour] shall not perish, but have eternal life.*

V17. For God did not send the Son into the world to judge and condemn the world [that is, to initiate the final judgement of the world], but that the world might be saved through Him.

V18. Whoever believes and has decided to trust in Him [as personal Saviour and Lord] is not judged [for this one, there is no judgement] no rejection, no condemnation; but the one who does not believe [that one has been convicted and sentenced], because he has not believed and trusted in the name of the [One and] only begotten Son of God [the One who is truly unique, the only One of His kind, the One who alone can save him].

My Salvation Story:

I knew about God from an early age because I was privileged to be raised by Christian parents. My walk with him has been marked with dependence, times of rebellion, especially in my teenage years, but thank God, His reins held me on and I did not fall too far off!

For the fact that I knew about God from a young age, I really did not know any other life than that of living as a 'Christian'. I enjoyed the company of Christians and kept Christian friends too, right from primary education through secondary and University years. I consciously surrendered the lordship of my life to God at age 19. This was when I reckon my personal walk with God actually started. I was an active member of the Christian Union Choir for most of my years in Medical School, University of Benin, Nigeria.

The depth of my walk with God became very real to me after my University years when I got married to a non- Christian man. My life became one of a roller coaster! And I feared for my life and my future. This made me quickly reconnect seriously with God. It was a matter of life and death, and I believed in my heart that only God could deliver me from the situation. Suffice to say, the marriage ended shortly after it started and I had to relocate to the United Kingdom in a most miraculous circumstances (this is a story for another day!)

At this time, I had three young boys and dedicated my life to raising them in the fear of God. All in all, I have come to learn that God, His Word (The person of Jesus Christ) and The Holy Spirit as the CONSTANT in the equation of my life. Always reliable and ever dependable!

I hope that my story may challenge you to have an enduring ongoing encounter with This Great Unchanging Changer, The Almighty God Whom you can recklessly trust with your entire life and you can be sure to smile because He alone can wrought the perfect **change** needed in every aspect of your life. Embracing His love and depending on His Word surely makes us enjoy peace and unmerited favour to walk confidently in this knowing.

Chapter 2

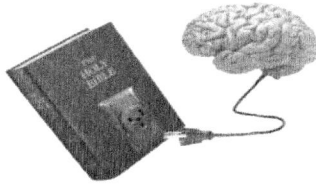

Change and Changing

C hange is a process, which most, if not all, of us do fear. It does not matter the nature of the change, either big or small. Internally, as in our thought patterns, behavioral patterns or attitudes or even materialistic (dreaming of a brand new home, or the latest model of your smartphone); it generates some form of anxiety. You and I know that change is imperative, because it is the very essence of all mechanisms in our universe. Thus change can be positive or negative depending on the influences. I believe that one of the characteristics of any living thing is change and being changed. Change is a factor, hard-wired into our DNA by the Creator in order for us to cope better with survival here on earth. The moment we choose not to embrace some form of change; we begin the slow but sure process of 'decay'. One of the fundamental characteristic elements of any living thing is dynamism; which involves emitting and contribution to the ecosystem; this in itself can be described as a form of change. Change is important and dynamic; thus needful for us to be and feel as living things. As you would agree, change is a very serious business!

2 Corinthians 5.17 (NKJV) "Therefore, if anyone is in Christ, he is a new creation; old things have passed away; behold, all things have become new.

We become new creatures after we have believed and said the prayers of salvation, hence we are said to be "born again". There is a need to embrace this change on every level. Our thoughts need to be transformed by the Word of God; because out of the abundance of our thoughts, we speak, and our habits and character is formed. The deeds then follow. A life experienced in God exudes the fragrance of Gods' love and mercy towards the self as well as to other people. If and when Gods word influences our thoughts, by extension, this also colours how we live our lives, every day, as new creation in Christ Jesus. Over time, our thoughts then align with Gods plan and purposes for us.

We, as humans, often times try to resist change consciously or unconsciously. It is important to consider why this is so; especially considering the first couple of decades of human existence is one of constant cellular growth and pre-programmed biochemical change. The template for our emotional growth also happens albeit in a malleable form (subject to be molded and transformed) with time.

Another dimension to change is the fact that there is change needed immediately on the intermediate and long term. Consciously or unconsciously, these processes are happening at varied paces for everyone. When we are aware of the process itself then we are able to appreciate the finer details of the change happening within us.

<u>MindWorkout Gym Exercise</u>:

The question we shall attempt to answer is – What is it about change that makes us anxious or fretful?

Why does the word CHANGE create an upsurge of such resistance in us?

A possible explanation is the fundamental fact that as human beings, we have come to learn by association that change is synonymous with unease; we associate any change with discomfort and/or pain. The idea is that this process will ultimately cause us discomfort. As soon as our brains make such associations and interpretations, our defense mechanisms kick in to protect our egos. This reaction often occurs unconsciously and much later consciously. So primarily, our defense mechanisms, (more often than not unconscious processes) kick off to resist the change process.

We dismiss the particular situation warranting change, even delete it, or better still alter the situation so that it can be more appealing to us. The extent to which we operate within our wall of defence mechanisms is dependent on our perception and appraisal of the situation; whether or not we deem it as a threat.

In Chemistry, heat brings about change in states, from solid to liquid and then gaseous state; matter evolves changing from one form to another. Likewise, we as humans undergo change by reason of our experiences; and if well- thought through, a positive change has the ability to enhance our lives in one way or another.

MindWorkout Gym Exercise:

Growth as a Christian comes about by daily transformation by the Word of God. What changes can you embrace so you can habitually engage God's Word to the extent that this change begins?

Take one habit at a time and develop a systematic plan to alter this habit to align with God's Word.

Set fifteen minutes aside every morning to talk to God and to listen to Him by reading the Bible more consistently.

Often, when change forces deep introspection, it warrants a stronger defensive response. Why? This could have some explanation such as fear of the unknown and association of the change process with painful consequences; thus we proceed to resist the process. As soon as the mind associates the change with pain, our defence mechanisms come up as oppositional barriers to resist it. So how we choose to perceive situations and process this determines how we are most likely to react. Such perceived threat creates unease and the emotion of fear sets in. Fear is a feeling or an emotion by which the body attempts to protect itself, from doing things that we have assumed to be dangerous; hence I define fear as the response to a perceived irrationally-unreal threat. Fear is highly subjective, because what can create the emotion of fear varies in the individual and also from one person to another.

Zig Ziglar describes "F-E-A-R as with two meanings: Forget Everything And Run or Face Everything And Rise. The choice is yours."

Here again the issue of choice comes in! The human brain upon perceiving fear, sends messages to the body to prepare for the natural response usually freeze, fight or flight. Physiological changes happen in our bodies and this makes us experience a collection of bodily signs and symptoms. Our brains can interpret these signs and symptoms in such a way that our bodies experience anxiety thus experiencing and feeling the emotion of anxiety in our bodies. In an effort to maintain status quo i.e. a state where we are not anxious, our brains can either dismiss and delete the situation, memory or thought, alter it to fit with what we desire or even find every reason in the world not to commence on such a potentially transformational journey.

This is one of the aims of this book - to assist you with embracing change painlessly. Life itself, like all energy, is dynamic, capable of transforming from one form to another; and as such, we cannot afford to be static. There are dire consequences such as missing our 'purpose'. We become stagnant and eventually it begins to feel as though we are moving backwards when indeed life is moving on and for all intents and purposes, we've been left behind.

In chapter One, we talked about a God Who made us in His image and likeness, Who imagined a beautiful and wonderful earth as against what was before Him - an earth without form and void and darkness upon it! If God made us in His likeness and image, are we not to see as

He sees? Hear as He hears? Feel as He feels and most importantly perceive our environment as He perceives? I will ask that you hold on to that thought for now.

Limiting Beliefs

Another possible explanation is the fear of the unknown. This can create such a response from our unconscious mind that ultimately inhibits us. The rationalizations we conjure in our minds may well be what is called limiting beliefs.

MindWorkout Gym Exercises:

When challenged beyond your comfort zones, can you truly say you faced the task fully with unbridled optimism? The inner voice of doubt likely casted the same fears we all have, but the message is the same: "I am not good enough".

When really, if one was to challenge oneself by questioning yourself as above, is your response to these doubts appropriate? Will my Father, God respond in this manner?

This is a typical example of a limiting belief. All of this starts with a thought, which almost immediately influences our physiology and vice versa. The mind and the body are linked, influencing one another in the most intricate manner. Our state of mind changes continually. As information passes through our senses to the mind, there is an appraisal and subsequent response message transmitted from the brain to the body; and this is one of the few things about it we can rely on. So yes, a lot happens at the thought level and indeed the thoughts we harbour in our minds determine who we are or indeed who we are becoming. The thoughts we habitually entertain and cultivate in our mind possess the ability to change electrical and chemical compositions in the brain. Over time, this can result in what we become. Depressed negative people or optimistic positive persons, the choice is yours! Proverbs 23:7 *"As he (man) thinketh in his heart so is he".* Our thoughts are powerful; your thoughts can make you or mar you. Our thoughts shape our choice of language use which then creates your world. Thoughts actively shape your world! God spoke in accordance to his thoughts; his desired imagination was of an orderly earth as against the one he was seeing - which was 'empty' and 'void'.

We are often more aware of our emotions than we are of our thoughts, physiology, posture, gesture and breathing patterns. These aspects of existence are not readily available to us; hence the need for us to be intentional. We do need to be consciously aware of these if we are to identify any problem areas; and thus embrace necessary adjustments to make the most of our minds as we embrace change.

Limiting Belief – What is it?

The origin and existence of limiting beliefs warrant some further investigation. A limiting belief is a subjective thought held with so strong a conviction that it is powerful enough to stall behaviour. They often come from a position of limited knowledge or even lack of understanding (or insight), which facilitates the depth to which humans can apply knowledge.

What the limiting belief does is to create a resistance that ultimately colours our perspectives and thus affects our choices and responses. It is becoming apparent that there is an aspect of our psyche that is engaged in processing of information without our conscious awareness. This process occurs so quickly and often we are unaware it is even happening. It could even be how we perceive and appraise situations, i.e. the perspective we choose. The perspective here refers to the 'lens' through which we view ourselves in relation to the outer world. The actual process of stalling an action or behaviour is a conscious one; however the driver of the limiting belief may not be readily available to our conscious minds. Hence, whatever action to correct the limiting belief has to comprise unconscious as well as conscious techniques, and we shall come to these later.

I believe that your decision to read this book is a willful decision done in the pursuit of knowledge, or at the very least to gain insight from another perspective. Acquiring knowledge leads to a better understanding of self and the surrounding world. Whichever well of understanding deepens, the individual has far more to gain from embracing change than rejecting it outright. Change is important in many aspects of life, approach all new information presented with an open mind to achieve a higher level of functioning, within the self, within the world and most importantly, with God.

An interesting and eye-opening exercise that I have read in Steven Covey's book "Seven Habits of Highly Effective People" will help us in this next section.

Taking the Inventory

At this moment, cast a long look into different aspects of your life that you are not fully satisfied with. As expected, there are various situations in the domains of life, which can do with some form of change. Change is essential at every strata; on the individual (personal) level, within the family and even within work organizations and society. Having agreed on the need for change, what we need to focus on now will be the management of this change so that our minds can embrace the change process painlessly.

What Actually Is Change?

Simply put, Change is a process (a series of small acts) which cumulatively, over time, brings about an outcome, an altered state. Human growth is the result of cell multiplication and differentiation regulated by the expression of genes. Mountains and cliff faces changes because of constant erosion by the sea, snow or rain. Change is a process through which something becomes altered in shape and functions differently too; it has a beginning, a middle section and an end.

The start of the change process within us begins with a realization that there is a state that is desired, but not attained in the present. The power of self-evaluation results in a heightened state of self- awareness; as well as the imagined state (dream) that is desired; and prepare the individual's mind for what is to come about; which is our expectation for the future. There is need for clarity of purpose with clear definitions of the present state and the dream (future expectation). A good level of understanding of these states provide us with the necessary tools needed for the middle stage.

The middle stage is the dynamic period that is crucial and often could be painful, because one may need to step out of their comfort zone to an unfamiliar one to learn more about why we are at our current position. Find and explore new strategies that may well be altering current thought patterns and behavioural steps involved in the change process. It is the ongoing processes of self-organization, emergence and re-emergence that characterize human systems. Important ingredients needed for this latter stage include, discipline and determination, a strong drive to keep the dream of your desired state in focus and alive. Willingness and flexibility to learn, as well as altering past knowledge and take on more and often new knowledge along the way that will ultimately bring us to making the dream or desire a reality.

The end section is achieving our desired outcome. To achieve an outcome, we need to have an idea of exactly what that is and how it will feel like when achieved. This is important so that when we attain the desired state, we may be able to comprehend that we have arrived at the desired outcome and better still, and hopefully not find this experience strange or even miss that desired state altogether.

As a process, each stage is co-dependent and as such we need to carefully take a closer look into what each stage entails because this will determine whether the desired outcome will be achieved or not.

Embracing change can be in the physical; in everyday

matters that our bodies are involved with. Psychologically in the realms of our thoughts, attitudes, behaviour, emotions and feelings that have a direct bearing on our minds or even our spirituality on some occasions.

The man's spirit is considered where the origin of life itself exists. Which makes perfect sense, if you remember that, at creation, God breathe into the nostrils of man for him to become a living soul (spirit). We mentioned that man was created to have a triune nature just like His Creator, God Himself. The human spirit, according to [8]Ellison 1993, pp.331- 332, is that which enables and motivates us to search for meaning or purpose in life, to seek the supernatural or something that transcends us, to wonder about our origins and our identities, to require mortality and equity. Stating that it is the spirit which synthesizes the total personality and provides an integrative force, Ellison also acknowledges that the spirit affects and is affected by the physical state, feelings, thoughts and relationships. If we are spiritually healthy, we feel generally alive, purposeful and fulfilled. This only extends to the state of our psychological health. Adding that, this relationship is bi-directional because of the intricacy between the different dimensions of the human (spirit, soul and body). Our spirit gets understanding, enlightenment and direction from the Spirit of the living God. So when man's spirit has light and feels well connected to The Spirit of God, and the Word of God, the mind and the body follow in the direction of being in harmony with one another.

The best analogy to describe this is with a house. If we built a beautiful castle, completely wired, roofed and with exotic décor, the only time you and others can enjoy the beauty of this castle will be during the day. At night-time when there is no power source, this very beautiful castle will be in total darkness. Therefore, except the wiring of this castle is connected to the National grid; there will be no electricity supply to it. So it is with the spirit of man. Every human has a spirit, whether this spirit is alive or not is dependent on whether that human spirit links with the Spirit of the living God. (When we say the prayer of salvation that is the initiating process of connecting our spirits with God's Spirit.) The beginning of a lasting relationship that transforms us inside out on a daily basis as we actively engage the Word of God.

Transforming The Mind

The very first lesson to learn is how to tune your mind more and more to the mind of God. "But how can I do this?" you may ask. Your mind perceives the environment through the windows of your senses. (Sense of sight, hearing, feeling, taste, smell and proprioception - an awareness of yourself in time and space). If your senses do not feedback into your mind, you will be cut off completely. So, in order to know how to adjust appropriately, we receive the messages through our sense, our brains interpret these and order necessary changes. Ultimately, our senses connect you to the world around you. By paying less attention to input from the external world via these senses, our spirits get more awakened and sensitive, then, we can tune more to the Spirit of God. This is a concept that is familiar to various religions, the concept of meditation, mindfulness, yoga, chanting among monks etc. are various ways people have developed connection with a Higher Being.

Being a Consultant Psychiatrist, my fascination remains with the working potential of the mind. The human mind has the ability to imagine, create images, dream states, scenes that often can make their way to reality; it does not matter the content of these. What is important is what you believe and what you say about your belief; how you craft the words that bring this belief to reality. It is thought that the human brain and the mind as well as the human body operate in a bidirectional manner. The mind though, with no physical location anatomically, exists in every human being. Studies have shown that there is a conscious and the unconscious aspects of the human mind. The conscious mind is largely the rational, logical aspect where our intellectual reasoning ability lies. We often operate in this realm most of our wakeful hours of the day. We think, recall memory and function intelligibly from this conscious wakefulness state. It is inextricably linked and bound by time.

The unconscious aspect of the mind is very much out of the alert wakefulness state. It is the aspect where our creativity lies. Our spirit operates largely in this realm and sadly, we often do not consciously access this. It is mostly operational when the physical senses are dulled. Many believe that our unconscious mind is the seat of unravelling very difficult and unresolved issues within the conscious. If not directed, the unconscious mind tends to deal on material that your conscious mind has considered the most; in other words, your most predominant thoughts of the day.

The unconscious mind is more operational when we are in a hypnotic state, half awake and half-asleep (drowsy) state and more so when we are asleep. Just like the mind receives information from the environment via all of our senses (sight, auditory, touch, taste, kinaesthetic, and smell), likewise our spirits can receive deep information/revelations from the Spirit of God at any time but we must be sensitive and also have the WORD of God; because often information from the Spirit of God which is downloaded into our spirits must align with God's Word. In a most complex interaction, this information influences not only the brain, but the spirit and the soul of man as well. This information becomes substrate for thought and character formation, as well as substrate for the unconscious mind to work with. Mixed with what we already have laid down by way of memory and past learning, the brain interprets the situation and the physical body responds by way of the feelings, emotions and behaviour generated.

Let's consider an illustration. Assuming you watched a horror movie with a friend. This friend from the cinema walked you home. That night as you slept, you had a dream and part of the scenes of the film becomes so real and intense. Your night sleep is disturbed. What has happened? Your unconscious mind has replayed the residue from the aspects of the horror movie that was of most significance to you when you watched the horror movie. As a rule, often the unconscious mind tends to dwell on and works on the most predominant thought within your conscious mind and the ones that emotionally affect or connect with you the most.

Often this also explains why when facing a difficult problem and you go to sleep with it on your mind, you may wake up with the perfect solution to the problem. Thoughts can be fleeting on your mind; however, the thoughts which you dwell upon the most or have the strongest emotional tone with tend to pass on to the unconscious mind for further processing. From the above description of the working of the mind and the scripture in Proverbs 23:7, it is evident that whatever predominant thoughts you bear in your mind colours the way your world is created and eventually becomes.

What is important are the thoughts you, as a person, allow to full maturity in your mind. The scriptures tell us that *as a man thinketh in his mind so is he*, in other words, whatever thoughts you allow to fill your mind the most and remain to fester, becomes, essentially, what you are becoming. Are you connecting the bits of the puzzle yet?

In a sense, our thoughts can affect our minds in profound ways that can either create or even limit us.

Faith Explained

The ability of the mind to create the predominant thoughts lies in the power of imagination and visualization crafted from the substrate of God's Word, its flexibility to adopt the unknown and often times explore untested grounds. The ability to see the substance of things hoped for long and hard enough until you see the evidence (the tangible details) of things not obvious to the physical senses in reality. The more this forms in your mind, the more motivation rises to make you take action to bring this formed imagination into reality.

This is what the Bible calls FAITH (see Hebrews 11:1). In the same chapter at Hebrews 11:6b, the scriptures clearly state that "without FAITH it is impossible to please God".

Believing and operating in the realms of FAITH described is an essential ingredient in making our desires, dreams, imaginations and aspirations manifest in the physical realm. The mind's ability to create lies upon its openness and willingness to embrace and question ideas in depth. It's ability to get motivated for the change process and ultimately the effrontery to dare embrace change that will make that dream come to reality – what a certain footwear conglomerate refers to as the 'just do it' attitude.

Take home message:

As humans, when we dream, we employ the powers of imagination and visualisation to soar beyond the limitations of our lives in reality into a wider world of possibilities. Riding on the wings of belief in God's Word is essential to pleasing God and bringing our dreams, imaginations and visualizations into REALITY. Accompanying dreams with necessary actions take us beyond ourselves to reach our desired outcomes. We must remain determined, focused and work smart. Dreams can turn into reality! It is all about embracing change which often times may not be comfortable.

MindWorkout Gym Exercise:

The power of imagination starts with our thinking ability. However, there has to be a substrate for our thoughts. This substrate directly derives from related facts from the word of God, or from the residue of all that your senses have fed into your mind all through a given period. The difference between the two sources is that while the Word of God has an inherent ability to feed into formed thoughts, imaginations, visualizations, the feedback via your senses often are full of negativity which can be disempowering. So choose carefully where you get your inspiration!

Learn to capture your thoughts, are they in keeping with Gods Word (Phil 4:8) Proper thought and Meditation should be: what is true, noble, just, pure, lovely and of good report. This holds the key to win the battle against worry.

Visualisation

Let's step further to visualizing a desired outcome. At this stage, you will need to create the exact image of what you desire and imbibe all the dimensions to it (the colour, intensity and texture and relevant details to the exact specific fit and feel the emotional tone and excitement associated to every imaginable detail of this desired outcome, consistency and shape in the right intensity and dimensions). Evaluate the often very huge differences between the present state and the desired state. The unconscious mind likes definite and specific images, created in the positive (affirmative). The ideas are expressed in the present tense. It needs to have the ability to associate benefits (feelings and emotions) with the desired state that are not associated with the present state, which may well be your reality.

You'll agree that many of us engage in this kind of exercise on a daily basis but to various extents. Some people with poor motivational drives end up being 'mere dreamers'. Mere dreamers just dream and they can dream fantastic ideas; however, these never materialize to reality. In order that these imaginations/visualizations, presuming they are positive and well formed, to materialize, there is the need for one's mind to maintain focus, persist with motivation and drive until this becomes real in your conscious world, in other words, until it becomes a reality.

There is a saying that goes "whatever the mind can conceive, it can achieve with accompanied hard work". That is true to an extent. There are mitigating factors why we are unable to embrace the necessary change to turn our dreams into reality. What could these be for you? As a Christian, the scriptures remind us that "we wrestle not against flesh and blood (physical elements) but against spiritual wickedness in high places" (Ephesians 6:12).

Every creation of God, including you and I, have a destiny and a destination in accordance to God's divine purpose and will; and this destiny is unique and personal for each of us. There is spiritual wickedness in high places that will stop at nothing to distract us and prevent us from reaching that beautiful ending. As spiritually-alive people of God, we are in a warfare that calls for 'spiritual weaponry'; because what we see in the physical is subject to change at the revelation of God's Word. The Word of God has the inherent dynamic ability to function as a sword in the spiritual realms as well as act as a powerful force in the physical; an effective weapon against the unseen spiritual battles we are involved in daily. Interestingly, God's Word remains the same forever, it is important to pray as though all effort to bring your dream to reality depends on God alone and work as though all effort lies with you (see Hebrews 11:6).

God has invested so much in us that we cannot but strive to a greater calling of improvement on every level in the life entrusted to our care. I am confident that the greater calling we have is to attain to all that God has created us to be. This realization should kick- start us into thinking of a desired state that is far better than our present state.

MindWorkout Gym Exercise:

Ask God to put godly outcomes in your mind if you cannot come up with any. If we ask, we are sure to get favourable answers, if we seek, we shall find and if we knock, the door shall be opened to us, that is a promise in God's Word (Matthew 7:7) we shall find and if we ask aright, we obtain from God our Father. Be awakened and let your mind go to work.

The Bible records Jesus saying in John 10:10 (KJV) "The thief cometh not, but for to steal, and to kill, and to destroy: I am come that they might have life, and that they might have it more abundantly." From this verse of scripture, it is obvious that our purpose is to live worshipfully to God, and enjoy this life abundantly in the process. This involves living this life to our full potentials.

However, because we have an adversary, the devil, who has a three-fold ministry to steal, kill and destroy, his army will unleash a spiritual attack on our minds to prevent us from making further progress with our godly desires or positive visualizations. This attempt can come in many ways but it is usually by unfruitful endeavours. When this happens, in the present, our joy and peace are robbed, as we are faced with a present physical life situation that takes up all our attention and focus away from God. Subsequently, we stop working hard at the process and on the longer term, instead we allow worry take hold and consume us; thus we end up not reaching the desired destination.

The secret to keep motivation up till your change comes lies in **making God your stronghold!** How we do this is by believing His Word above all else and against any other evidence before us.

The English dictionary defines a stronghold as "a defensive structure". Psalms 9:9 describes the LORD as a refuge for the oppressed, a stronghold in times of trouble. This is the inaccessible place, figuratively, a refuge, and a defense. We build such spiritual defensive structure by choosing to meditate daily and habitually on the word of God; by engaging habitual prayers using the Word of God in prayers.

Learning to Pray Effectively

This is one spiritual way to embrace your change. There is a spiritual realm as much as a physical realm exists. We need to know how to operate effectively in the spiritual realms as what we see in the physical already exist in the spiritual realms which is not readily available to us but can, however, be felt by us. In other words, the spiritual realm (that which we do not see) controls the physical (that which we see and know as reality).

A renowned Bible teacher and man of God, Pastor E. A. Adeboye, in his book "The Mathematics of Answered Prayers", explained prayer in an equation as follows:

$$F (P + W + R + JN) = \text{Answered Prayers}$$

Faith (F) is the Constant variable that must affect other elements of your equation before your prayers can be answered. (Hebrews 11:6 says *"without faith it is impossible to please God: for he that cometh to God must believe that He is and that He is a rewarder of them that diligently seek Him"*).

Faith is the essential and most crucial element in prayers!

The next essential element is P (Praise) because this attracts God's attention Psalm 100:4 (*"Enter into His gates with thanksgiving, And into His courts with praise, Be thankful to Him, and bless His name"*).

The next element is W (Word of God) which is the reference base upon which the prayers rest. The evidence to present in backing your prayers. So before you bring your prayers to God, first you must search for what God's word says about the prayer requests, in that way, you do not ask amiss. (James 4:3)

R stands for the Request you have which must be specific, smart, measurable and well formed. For example, bless me Lord is loose and non-specific. What particular blessing are you asking for? We need to state this in the present form.

Lastly, JN – Jesus Name. Every request must be

presented to The Father in Jesus' name. When you pray in the name of Jesus, you are placing the personality of Jesus behind your request and since God cannot deny Jesus anything, He will not deny you either. He will attend to your request just as He attends to the request of Jesus. Col 1:19 says, *"for it pleased God that in Christ Jesus should all fullness dwell"*. And Jesus said in John 14:6 [NKJV] Jesus said to him, *"I am the way, the truth and the life. No one comes to the Father except through Me")*

John 4:13 (NKJV) *"And whatever you ask in my name, that I will do, that the Father may be glorified in the Son"*.

John 15: 7 (NKJV) *"If you abide in Me and my words abide in you, you will ask what you desire, and it shall be done for you"*.

John 16: 24-76 (NKJV) *"Until now, you have asked nothing in My name. Ask, and you will receive, that your joy may be full. These things I have spoken to you in figurative language, but the time is coming when I will no longer speak to you in figurative language, but I will tell you plainly about the Father. In that day, you will ask in My name, and I will do say to that I shall pray the Father for you; for the Father Himself loves you, because you have loved Me, and have believed that I come forth from God"*.

MindWorkout Gym Exercises:

Try to use the Prayer equation to develop a template of prayers concerning issues you wish to pray about. Keep a journal of your prayers and remember to return to write when your prayers are answered. (This is a good exercise that will build your faith)

Chapter 3

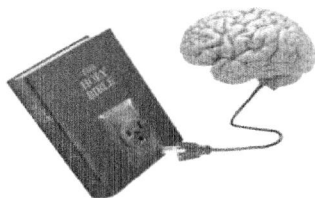

Knowing Your Identity

Knowing your identity in God, your position and place in the spiritual realms becomes crucial in this process of change. As a Bible-believing Christian, you are rooted in the righteousness of Jesus Christ. You are created with what it takes to prevail in spiritual warfare. Knowing your identity gives you confidence to explore and be comfortable in your walk. Knowing your identity helps you prioritize and seek for clarity when you think you may not be on course.

My sons know beyond doubt that, at any time, they can approach me to ask for anything because they know it is their right to. No matter how long any guest stays in my house, that fact alone cannot make that stranger have the same rights and entitlements as my sons. If my sons did not know that they are my children, they may have doubt as to whether to come to me or not. Nevertheless, because we have a relationship, they have the boldness to do so. Likewise, we need to know our identity in God. I see God as my Father and I relate with Him on such basis. I speak to Him about my feelings whether good or bad. I tell him my dissatisfaction with the stage I am at and where I would like to be. I ask Him to help my desires align to His will and purposes in accordance to His Word for my life.

Knowing your identity comes from deep within. I am not ashamed to come before God with my feelings and emotions, which I cannot share with any other human because I fear they may judge me. You see knowing my identity in God underpins the quality and depth of relationship that I have with God the Father. You can develop that too! Apart from helping you face difficult situations or giving you direction when you think you may have missed your way, this knowledge gives you immense confidence to walk the Christian life boldly because you know you have a loving relationship with a Father, the Maker of the heavens and the earth to whom you can be accountable. You know that you can come before God with anything whatsoever (even when you utterly fail and fall) and you will not be ashamed. This is so because Romans 8:1 (NKJV) says, *"There is therefore now no condemnation to them who are in Christ Jesus who walk not after the flesh, but after the Spirit"*.

Condemnation Undermines Confidence

While scripture encourages us to come boldly before God's presence to obtain grace and find help in time of need in (Hebrews 4:16), the typical way the enemy makes us feel unworthy to enter God's presence is to remind us of some wrong doing (sins of omission or commission); this is the condemnation that is referred to in Romans 8:1. The Bible refers to Satan as the accuser of the brethren and the father of lies. Jesus came and perfectly paid the price for all our sins, once and for all, with His blood which He shed on the cross over two thousand years ago. This act of Jesus was because of God's love for us. We may not understand how or why God so loved us but it is important for us to accept this love, embrace the eternal provision that makes God's mercy to override every judgement of the enemy against us. On a fundamental basis, you must know your identity i.e. get to truly understand and know who you are in Christ Jesus! Once you have a relationship with God, maintaining that relationship is not by our human effort but rather by the grace of God in which we walk in accordance with the leading of the Holy Spirit – a free gift from God to all who ask. Romans 8:14 says *as many that are led by the Spirit of God are the sons of God.*

This is important because on a daily basis there are issues we struggle with when it comes to maximizing our lives. Our dependency on God, His Spirit and His Word will provide every deep understanding of the grace (unmerited favor) that is needed and available to overcome such struggles and every form of condemnation suggested by the devil.

These could be in the area of our thoughts, attitudes, emotions and ultimately some behaviour such as addictions. These struggles tend to limit our ability to enjoy life to the fullest; primarily because these have a peculiar way of limiting our ability to exercise our minds, to stretch it beyond our limitations, or to even question how we think, why we behave the way we do and decision making processes resulting in choices we make daily. Thus, our minds do not expand to any extent beyond what we can feel, taste, see, smell and hear (the physical realm). John 17:3 (NKJV) "And this is eternal life, that they may know You, the only true God, and Jesus Christ whom You have sent" Everyone will live eternally somewhere, but for those of us who BELIEVE, the eternal life Jesus spoke about here means living forever in Gods' presence. Eternal life is not just referring to length of life but a healthy quality of life; one in which we know God as our Lord, our Father and our closest friend; a life free of addictions and limiting beliefs; indeed a fulfilling life of walking in right standing with God, of peace and joy in the Holy Ghost.

Strongholds

These are spiritual states that limit us from being all that God has created us to be. These states of being can be living with various forms of addictions.

The Oxford English Dictionary defines a Stronghold as:

1. A place fortified against attack.
2. A place of strong support for a cause or political party.

Strongholds can be positive or negative anchors on which our thoughts, attitudes, and behaviour emerge. Strongholds may exist as thought patterns, attitudes, emotional states or even behaviour that tend to rule our lives via the mind beyond our conscious control. We often feel so helpless and feel as though we are at their mercy. Remember earlier, I mentioned the need to anchor your life in God, making HIM your STRONGHOLD; yes? That is a positive and good stronghold. Most matured Christians have, through practice and due diligence, attained to this state. However, a mind that is not wholly submissive to the authority and effective ruling of the Word of God is most susceptible to the manipulations of the enemy that can create negative strongholds existing in the spiritual realm.

Mechanism of Stronghold Formation

The Bible tells us that the enemy of our soul is Satan, the father of lies. He is crafty and in a subtle way creates situations of FEAR (False Experiences Appearing Real). This often, but not always, is in the form of a thought emerging from a past, present or imagined future experience. This thought, if not appropriately dealt with by the Word of God, can fester and over a period become believable as REAL to the individual.

An experiential example:

When my marriage ended in divorce, I made up my mind that even though I was now single, I would not defile myself and sleep around. Indeed I still hold true to that; and the enemy keeps making one compelling argument after another (to break it) in my thought processes. Many women in my position have fallen for the devil's trick that may go somewhat like this: 'Surely God cannot be angry with you if you use sex toys to satisfy your physiological needs. And for as long as you are not engaging in fornication and adultery, that is OK'. They justify themselves and become enslaved and addicted to certain practices such as use of sex toys or having "friends with benefits" just for the sake of meeting their physiological needs. Well not that I advocate that use of sex toys is right or wrong, but the aspect that I am emphasizing here is the hold that such practices have on the individual over time.

You may not see any problem with what I've described above but I pray that God will open your eyes to the folly and danger of doing this. If you've already fallen prey to it, you need to pray for forgiveness and ask for mercy, deliverance and grace from God. The Deliverer Himself will take up your case and set you free from any such bondages, amen!

What may start out just as a thought, can become a stronghold that will hold you captive for years and limit your enjoyment of God's inheritance for you. Yes, I am not married again, but I have such peace with God and I am enjoying full fellowship with the council of the Trinity because I made a choice to remain obedient to God and His Word. I always pray for unusual grace to maintain my chastity and that has been my story ever since. I am forever grateful to God that He is my STRONGHOLD. I rely on His power on a daily basis to remain an overcomer in Christ Jesus.

Mind you, there is no way you can overcome these strongholds with your physical will power. You need to tune your spirit to the Spirit of God in order to obtain specific instructions (which often align to the word of God in the Bible) on how to overcome them.

With each passing day, an individual with negative strongholds becomes incapable of exerting any control over their minds, thoughts, impulses and actions. If one allows them to prevail, the strongholds become fortified against the transformational power of God's Word. This is because over time, they have subdued the sense of good and evil; thus overpowered the unconscious mind of such an individual. As you know, the unconscious mind is every human's seat of creativity. The unconscious is also believed to be the source of our imaginations.

To begin the process of change, we need to think of where we are presently, where we wish to be (the desired state) and the process (the 'how' to move from the former to the latter)! The patterns of thought we entertain determines whether we get there or not. There are healthy, positive thought patterns and there are unhealthy, negative thought patterns. Our thought patterns over time colour our lives. In a way, thought patterns determines the 'real person' an individual becomes.

I will illustrate this phenomenon in a naturally occurring process within the body. The human body has an elaborate antioxidant defense system. Antioxidants are manufactured within the body and can be extracted from the food, we humans eat; such as fruits, vegetables, seeds, nuts, meats, and oil. Free radicals are released during the process of oxidation in the body. These free radicals then proceed to cause chain reactions that oftentimes are toxic within the physical body. There are certain chemicals called antioxidants (meaning "against oxidation") which work to protect lipids from peroxidation by radicals. Antioxidants are effective because they are willing to give up their own electrons to free radicals. When a free radical gains the electron from an antioxidant it no longer needs to attack the cell and the chain reaction of oxidation is broken. After donating an electron, an antioxidant becomes a free radical by definition. Antioxidants in this state are not harmful because they have the ability to accommodate the change in electrons without becoming reactive. The human body has an elaborate antioxidant defense system. Antioxidants are manufactured within the body and can be extracted from the food humans eat such as fruits, vegetables, seeds, nuts, meats, and oil.

In the same way, we can liken the free radicals from process of oxidation as the by-products of all the stuff we choose to feed our mind through our senses. As is often the case, these have not been modified and they can cause chain reactions resulting in toxic habits that are contrary to the ways and will of God. When we take in the antioxidants of the Word of God, this will help us modify those harmful free radicals to non-harmful free radicals. Only God and His Word have the power, the dynamic ability to bring about change in any area of our lives.

Mindworkout Gym Exercise:

Prayerfully locate the right scripture relevant to the problem area you are struggling with and apply the word appropriately. Replacing the habit generating thought with the thoughts based on the truth of God's Word. Create positive affirmations and recite these anytime the 'bad' thoughts intrude your mind.

Hebrews 4:12 (CEV) describes in details the potency of this Word of God. It says "God's word is ALIVE and POWERFUL! It is sharper than any double-edged sword. His WORD can cut through our spirits and souls and through our joints and marrow, until it discovers the desires and thoughts of our hearts."

Start believing, thinking and speaking right. Think before you speak; think before you act!

You have nothing to lose by depending on the Spirit of God to help modify (bring about change of) the habits you have formed that are now controlling you.

Proverbs 23:7 says *"For as he thinks in his heart, so is he."* A thought pattern can become so deeply ingrained that it works either for you or against you. Just as negative thought patterns have the power to resist change; positive thought patterns equally have the ability to make our goals change for the better and thus make us dream-achievers.

I prescribe medication to treat the symptoms my patients bring to the consulting room. Unfortunately, I cannot confidently say that these medicines have the potency that the Word of God has in reaching to the core of certain issues that pertain to the soul and spirit of a man. The tablets I prescribe do not have the power or efficacy to transform or renew the mind, neither do they have the ability to divide asunder the soul and spirit (the very core of the person) of the human mind; I must mention that indeed the medication often help to correct some chemical imbalances which result in symptom presentation of mental disorders however. The approaches to human problems need to be tackled from the realms of the spirit soul and body using known remedies that actually have potency to bring about lasting change.

Medication have expiration dates but the Word of God never does! It will never ever fail.

Romans 12:1-2 (AMP) puts it this way: *Therefore I urge you, brothers and sisters, by the mercies of God, to present your bodies [dedicating all of yourselves, set apart] as a living sacrifice, holy and well –pleasing to God, which is your rational (logical, intelligent) act of worship. 2. And do not be conformed to this world [any longer with its superficial values and customs] but be TRANSFORMED and PROGRESSIVELY changed [as you mature spiritually] by the renewing of your mind [focusing on godly values and ethical attitudes] so that you may prove [for yourselves what the will of God is, that which is good and acceptable and perfect [in His plan and purpose for you].*

Positive thought patterns can be born out of the reality of God's word. They are infused with power from on high and capable of overcoming all negativity, unproductiveness as well as negative strongholds of the enemy. Remember, how the Spirit of God moved upon the face of the waters to make God's spoken Word come to life at Creation? Just in the same way, God's Spirit can move in your peculiar situation to help bring about change in your life too; however, you need believe, think and speak the WORD of God for the Spirit to work on!

In embracing change painlessly, you will agree with me that it is important then to know how to identify and deal with any negative strongholds.

Identifying Negative Strongholds

The process of identifying unhealthy or negative strongholds in one's life may be easy or difficult. The ease with which it comes across to you depends on how much you have firstly embraced the Word of God. The Word of God, by its nature, quickens your spirit to identify strongholds for what they are. The Holy Spirit then empowers you with the will power to effectively deal with them through prayers as we've seen earlier. More importantly, the change can only come about by how much your spirit have allowed the Word of God to transform your thought processes.

In the everyday workings of the mind, there is a need to believe the Word of God concerning us; as the only truth and final arbiter! The only truth, period! With time, this will influence our everyday thoughts and eventually influence our character and our way of life.

Genesis 37 tells us of the story of Joseph, the son of Jacob, the great grandson of Abraham. Joseph was a young man many of us can relate with today. He learnt through very bitter experiences to develop a trusting relationship with God, he learnt how to embrace the Word of God from an early age to identify some negative strongholds (trusting flesh, pride, and boasting of God's plan revealed to him in dreams) to bring about change in his life. He gradually moved from a young lad who by all standards, a superficial man, to a 'deep' spiritual man who saw the world through the eyes of the scripture – the Word of God. Trusting and fearing God with Whom he had developed a strong dependable relationship in the depths of his being. Through every adverse experience, he learnt obedience and humility as well as coming to an understanding of where his stronghold should be - in the reverential fear of the everlasting God. When one attains to a place of anchoring to God alone, living everyday life as a Christian becomes so much easier. And one does not need to fight with negative strongholds with the flesh anymore.

Strongholds can exist in very many ways, singly or in varied combination, in an individual's life. Examples of some common strongholds include jealousy, insecurity, lust, greed, anxieties or irrational fears, which can lead on to persistent, low self-esteem, lying, unbelief, ungodly thoughts and various forms of addictions. Addictions to pornography, sex, sex toys, alcoholism, acquisition of material things; addiction to smoking cannabis or other illicit substance use; and many more. The impact of these in people's lives varies in terms of severity. One man's stronghold may be lack of control when it comes to making choices; while in another, it may be inability to take charge of the directional flow of affairs in their lives.

Negative strongholds are identified by their destructive abilities. Initially they are simply referred to as habits, which people may even proudly talk about. Over time, these gradually begin to cause havoc in different aspects of the individual's life such that the individual loses all self-control, and eventually end up in states where their minds become enslaved. They feel compelled to act in obeisance to the negative thoughts or desires. Often these habitual patterns may be actions and behaviour that one would not normally exhibit or would be ashamed to be seen doing. This compulsion becomes so strong thus controlling their emotions, feelings and impulses.

With time, the individual lacks total control in stopping or modifying such destructive behaviour and thus may end up even in the criminal justice system; or in the loss of pivotal relationships- losing custody of their children or their spouses walking out on them. Despite head knowledge of the consequences and knowing what is right to do, the person with strongholds, when faced with situations, ends up making decisions and choices that are against the appropriate and rightful thing to do over and over again. Such persons make choices that are evidently harmful to their physical body, spiritual being and ultimately even their loved ones.

MindWorkout Gym Exercise:

You may just be wondering whether you have a negative stronghold or strong 'deep' character or you may even ask yourself, how can I free myself from a negative and life-limiting stronghold?

You will need to develop sensitivity to God, His Spirit and the Word of God. Being sensitive to the Spirit of God is not enough in itself; you will need to be willing and obedient to do whatever the Word of God asks of you in faith, believing that God is able to save and deliver.

Developing sensitivity to God, His Spirit and the Word of God starts with all humility and total reliance on God's Word. When we come to God asking and seeking, we always find answers because He is a faithful God. To him that knocks, the door shall be opened. (Matt 7:7; 1st John 5:14-15)

Pray, as I described earlier, that God by His Spirit will reveal to you any negative strongholds that may be in your life. Trust that God is capable of giving you every strength to overcome this stronghold; and it does not matter how long the stronghold might have limited you; just believe, trust God and obey His Word. By this, you can gain sufficient insight into identifying certain internal and external environmental cues to avoid or abstain from.

I have heard some persons pray prayers such as make me sick Lord at the thought of alcohol or cannabis or whatever substances they are addicted to and believing this prayers from the heart and trusting Gods ability; it happens in reality and over time, this nausea drives a wedge between the person and the substance and they are eventually delivered!

Some strongholds can exist in more subtle forms e.g. procrastinations, slothfulness (a disinclination to work or exert yourself), always making excuses and being indecisive or even wasting time. Even though these may not have immediate consequences, they have the potential to prevent you from taking appropriate action in time to embrace necessary change that will bring you closer to your desired outcome.

One typical characteristic of most strongholds is that they ultimately steal your joy in everyday living. They steal your sense of inner satisfaction, peace and inner rest. Ultimately, they can even destroy a life given enough time. Absolutely nothing is worth taking your peace, joy and your daily enjoyment of walking and fellowship with God.

<u>MindWorkout Gym Exercise</u>:

You may now, probably, be able to outline some unhelpful negative strongholds that exist in your life. Why not list and write them down and ask God in prayers to give you the ability to overcome these?

To rid yourself from a stronghold, firstly you need to evaluate every aspect of your life (using the wheel of life, freely available on Google search) to identify any such stronghold mentioned earlier. Genuinely seek to understand how and why these have come about and how these are hindering forces in your life. You may wish to study biblical characters and learn from their stories. Insight often drops in your spirit during such moments!

The next stage is to intently search for specific scriptures that address your situation and create affirmations based upon the Word of God. Use these affirmations prayerfully, daily, to get rid of them.

What is the Word of God?

Hebrews 4:12-13 (AMPC) describes it like this:

"For the Word that God speaks is alive and full of power [making it active, operative, energizing, and effective]; it is sharper than any two-edged sword, penetrating to the dividing line of the breath of life (soul) and [the immortal] spirit, and of joints and marrow [of the deepest parts of our nature], exposing and sifting and analyzing and judging the very thoughts and purposes of the heart.

13 And not a creature exists that is concealed from His sight, but all things are open and exposed, naked and defenseless to the eyes of Him with Whom we have to do."

The Word of God is a mirror by which we see our true nature. It enables us to see our outward and inward spiritual states. If we say that the Word of God is a mirror as alluded in James 1:23-25 below, then we need to trust its ability to examine our thoughts, actions and attitudes; to expose what needs to change as well as be willing to replace the unhealthy thought patterns that are in the present sufferings.

"For if anyone is a hearer of the word and not a doer, he is like a man observing his natural face in a mirror; 24 for he observes himself, goes away, and immediately forgets what kind of man he was. 25 But he who looks into the perfect law of liberty and continues in it, and is not a forgetful hearer but a doer of the work, <u>this one will be blessed in what he does.</u>" - (James 1:23-25).

Once you identify these strongholds, realize that you have the ability to respond accordingly, which is one reason why this book is about taking on responsibility by embracing change painlessly and by God's way!

There are physical and spiritual components to your response because scriptures clearly tells us in 2 Corinthians 10:3-6 (KJV):

"For though we walk in the flesh, we do not war after the flesh: **(For the weapons of our warfare are not carnal, but mighty through God to the pulling down of strongholds;)** *Casting down imaginations, and every high thing that exalteth itself against the knowledge of God, and bringing into captivity every thought to the obedience of Christ; and having in a readiness to revenge all disobedience,*

when your obedience is fulfilled."

Two Useful Ways For Dealing With Strongholds

Firstly, seeking professional help from secular world. There are many trained therapists who can offer man's knowledge and help.

Secondly, by distracting your mind; and prayerfully searching appropriate knowledge base from God's Word to help overcome these. Please note that this should not replace seeking professional help when necessary.

Once you believe that you have these spiritual warfare tools, apply them to your thought patterns on a daily basis. For example, when the familiar thoughts that invade your mind before you engage in watching pornography enters your mind, you identify these and name it specifically by name. For example, you can say:

"You spirit of pornography I come against you by the power in the Name of Jesus. At the Name of Jesus every knee should bow and every tongue confess that Jesus Christ is Lord to the glory of God the Father; I cast you, spirit of pornography, down right now and I free my mind to the Spirit of the Living God. I speak wholesome thoughts in my mind and I declare the Word of God to flood my thoughts by Your Spirit right now, in Jesus Name, Amen."

You may need to consciously do this many times till your thoughts begin to switch almost immediately. You then move away from the triggers and chose to listen to either the audio Bible, gospel music or words that will lift your spirit and tune it to the Spirit of God. With time, you will become free of these strongholds, you will need to rely on God's Word for the ability to maintain the 'changed you' to remain that way.

Commit to regular and consistent study of the Word of God on a daily basis to realign your thoughts to be in keeping with God's ways.

So far, we have come to see that strongholds are set and established in the mind. They can neither be seen nor be touched because they exist in the spirit realm. Hence, mere physical actions are not enough. However, we can effectively deal with these strongholds by using specific spiritual weaponry, which include – prayers in your understanding as well as prayers in the Spirit; appropriate application of the Word of God, which is the sword of the Spirit, and seeking spiritually-inclined persons who can mentor you as well to whom you can become accountable physically.

Establishing God's Word: The truth-base by which to pull down strongholds

In order to wage a war, you must have a base and a place to launch your attacks. This base has to be secure and with the necessary proven impact ability. That base is the truth contained in God's Word, which equates the sword of the Spirit. (Ephesians 6:17).

Another effective way to use the Word of God in this warfare is to use it as the gold standard by which every thought and imagination that enters the mind is measured against. If such thoughts/imaginations/images do not align with scriptures and the purpose of God in your life, you must get rid of them immediately in accordance with the above scripture and prayer pattern. When any ungodly thought or desires intrude upon your mind, you need to check them against Philippians 4:8 which says:

"Finally believers, whatsoever is true, whatever is honorable and worthy of respect, whatever is right and confirmed by God's Word, whatever is pure and wholesome, whatever is lovely and brings peace, whatever is admirable and of good repute: if there is any excellence, if there is anything worthy of praise, think continually on these things [center your mind on them, and implant them in your heart]".

So ask yourself, are these good and wholesome thoughts according to the judgment of God's Word?", or are they ephemeral/canal thoughts (selfish and destructive). If these thoughts are indeed carnal, then you take such thought intrusions captive immediately dismissing them by pulling them down using your weapon "The Word of God". For example, say:

"You thought of lust, I rebuke you in the name of Jesus"

Ask for the Lord's strength to keep them out of your conscious mind. You may pray in this manner or as you deem fit:

"Father in the Name of Jesus, I plead the blood of Jesus over my mind and I subject my will to the Lordship of Jesus Christ".

You can repeat this prayer as many times as possible and each time place emphasis on the fact that you are a covenant child of God standing upon the righteousness of Jesus Christ. Persist until you believe that you have the ability to instantly dismiss undesirable thoughts from your mind and fill your mind with more appropriate thoughts that are wholesome, uplifting and edifying. Remember that initially it may seem nothing is happening, I admonish you to persevere and persist. The negative thought patterns did not become strongholds overnight; it took a while; so the change will happen with and in time. Just believe that God's Word has the capability to bring about the necessary change.

Realize that your mind is the battleground where the attacks take place. You need to guard it with all diligence. This is done by closely monitoring the kind of materials that you feed it e.g. the quality of what you watch, hear, feel or smell. For instance, if you have problems with lustful thoughts and pornography, it will not be wise to watch naked or half nude girls on TV or watch films with nudity and the like. Your senses are the windows to your mind!

Take the responsibility of intentionally distracting yourself by searching more closely the Word of God. Just as a baby starts out by drinking milk and is weaned, so also you will need to train your mind to embrace change using the Word of God and prayers as your weaponry until you reach a state of discipline. Habits formed are difficult to break; however, your determination and dependency on the Spirit of God can help you overcome any addictions and habits.

Now I want to use this analogy to drive this message home even more. If you have an infection and you are prescribed a course of antibiotics, you take the medication as prescribed and for the entire duration in order to get the maximum benefit, which is to get rid of the infection. What happens if you do not take the medication as prescribed? The infection will remain and even may become a super bug that will be very difficult to treat later. Likewise, failing to use the Word of God appropriately and consistently may result in the strongholds becoming more difficult to rid. You need to take a daily dose of the Word of God to renew your mind (Romans 12:1-3). This is where, memorizing scripture and committing such to mind is crucial! The inner transformation can only happen by you making the effort to search the scriptures.

Memorizing the scriptures, pondering, meditating on the scriptures, muttering and thinking on the scriptures, speaking the scriptures day and night; and by prayers (praying in your understanding and in the Spirit) that the Holy Spirit will empower as well as quicken the Word of God in your life to bring about needed change.

Steadfastly remain rooted in God's Word because your mind is the battleground for the spiritual warfare referred to earlier. Moment by moment, you need to be able to keep tabs with what is going on in your mind. Just like attending the physical Gym brings benefit over a period of consistent attendance and engagement in the programme drawn by your fitness instructor, likewise, the mind needs daily exercising by using scriptures in what I term 'mind workout gym'. There is the need for you to continue to anchor your mind with the appropriate ammunition. As soon as you stop restocking, the enemy will start closing in and before long, you can end up being seized by even stronger, overbearing strongholds.

2 Timothy 2:15 says *"Study to shew thyself approved unto God, a workman that needeth not to be ashamed, rightly dividing the word of truth."* (KJV)

"Study and do your best to present yourself to God approved, a workman [tested by trial] who has no reason to be ashamed, accurately handling and skillfully teaching the Word of truth." (AMP)

If the mind perceives that the benefits associated with the desired outcome outweighs that of the present state, then it is empowered to persevere with the difficult middle process of learning new habits to replace older unhealthy ones; as well as unlearning some older habits we may have become so used to.

There is pain associated with change. The pain may be psychological, emotional, financial or even acceptance that the present state has been managed poorly. Accepting the latter aspect is about taking on personal responsibility. So what exactly does this mean you may ask? I believe this concept is accepting that you have the inherent ability to choose and respond appropriately in any peculiar situation. Each of us has this ability in us. So for our spiritual wellbeing, we need to embrace spiritual activities so we can enjoy life full and in a balanced way.

The World Health Organization defines health as a state of complete physical, mental and social wellbeing and not merely the absence of disease or infirmity. For a moment, let us pause and ponder on this definition!

The Oxford definition of health is the state of being

free from illnesses or injury and wellbeing as a state of being comfortable healthily (be in good health) or happy – physical and mental). You and I know that the human mind is far much more complex than just being comfortable healthily, there is a spiritual dimension that drives all of our human endeavours. This is the very reason why tackling the state of mental well-being, we need to consult the owner's manual – The BIBLE. God made the human body as an intricately delicate structure that can be as resilient as well as undergo so much change through the effects of STRESS.

Chapter 4

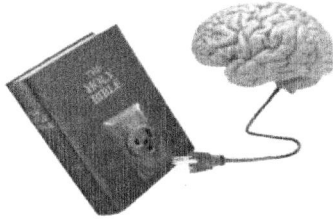

Emotional Intelligence

How does it feel when people ask an adult a question like "are you talking with the benefit of common sense?"; or "are you listening to yourself at all?" I have found myself asking a few people these questions not out of spite but as an effort to kick-start some self-evaluation. On each occasion, I truly wonder how many times we actually process our thoughts, think before we speak or even consider the effect of our words on the hearers before letting them out. It is true that some thoughts are better kept as thoughts and to ourselves.

It often baffles me that many people grow up without learning from a young age how to think before speaking or think before acting. Insensitive comments and careless use of words pierce others to create wounds that heal slowly if they ever do. A thinking man is, most of the time, a self-evaluator.

To be a self-evaluator, it is good practice to process our words in our minds and weigh this against God's Word as directed in Philippians 4:8. Then and only then, can we evaluate how much of those words are worth sharing with others. Our words are powerful and have the potential to build, and create or tear down and destroy. You make the choice as to which your words will be. Even when we have to criticize others, let us be careful to critic positively and build up instead of tearing down our hearers. The book of Proverbs beautifully puts it that *"the mouth of the righteous is a well of life.... but the mouth of the foolish is near destruction".* Let us strive for our mouths to be as that of the righteous; a mouth that gives life, grace and hope to the hearers at all times. Consider the following verses:

Colossians 4:6: *"Let your speech be always with grace, seasoned with salt, that ye may know how ye ought to answer every man."*

Ephesians 4:29 also says: *"Let no corrupt communication proceed out of your mouth, but that which is good to the use of edifying, that it may minister grace unto the hearers."*

From the above scriptures, it is clear that we are to take the responsibility of watching what we say. If we constantly make the choice to think before we speak, then we have won the greatest of all battles – control of the mouth. Sometimes we err, but self-evaluation enables us to keep that monster of a thing called 'the tongue', in check. I believe God gave us two ears and one mouth for a purpose. Always think before speaking, it will make you sound wise and stand out as a man (or woman) of understanding. Even when jesting, be careful. If that is an area of weakness for you, then learn to tune your spirit to the Spirit of God when you are in the circles of jesters and you will find that the words you contribute are wholesome. It is never too late to start the process of self-reflection and self-evaluation. This can be a measure of your emotional intelligence.

What Is Emotional Intelligence?

Intelligence to the human does involve many aspects and emotional intelligence is an aspect that is extremely important to the average human.

There has been unparalleled burst of scientific studies in the area of human emotions. I personally believe that emotional intelligence is the crucial ingredient necessary to complement our intellects. The spice that makes the difference in the taste of life and living!

Just what does this mean? I could not agree less with Daniel Goleman, a renowned psychologist who wrote a book on Emotional intelligence. He describes genetic heritage as "that which endows each of us with a series of emotional set points that determines our temperament and that academic intelligence has little to do with emotional life".

Emotional intelligence is the set of abilities (or traits) which enable us to motivate ourselves and persist in the face of huge frustrations, to **exercise** our minds; thinking rationally and **modulate** our impulses; **delaying gratification** and most importantly to be **able to step into another person's shoes** to view any situation from as many perspectives as possible. Emotional intelligence is the ingredient that characterizes well-rounded people and can be described as maturity in layman's terms.

I like to consider emotional intelligence as that quality that adds a measure of depth to your personality. The human mind was created to be in submission to the human spirit, which was created to be in submission to the Spirit of God, the Holy Spirit. You have the responsibility to tame your mind to be in submission to your spirit which should be in total submission to the Spirit of God.

Reading thus far, you may be wondering if all of this is not just a bit too abstract. Bear with me; and I dare say that it is a good thing to wonder. Even though it may sound rather abstract at this stage, I shall endeavor to drive my message home quite soon.

Supposing you have worked in an organization for ten years and you hold some level of responsibility as a regional supervisor. Deep down you wish you could become area manager because you know that you have the skills and competence to do the job possibly better than the incumbent area manager does. What will you do? There is clearly a process of evaluation that has occurred, perhaps even in your unconscious mind. You have created a desired state in your mind (becoming an area manager).

There are obvious benefits associated to this desired state, which may be of more worth to those associated to regional supervisor (your present state). Will you continue diligently with your work and hope that one day the boss will notice your good work and dilligence? Or will you become a back stabber and do all within your means to discredit the incumbent area manager just to get them sacked so you can take the position at all costs? A moral dilemma, some may think, but for a person who truly knows God as a Father will do the former and not the latter. They will work conscientiously while waiting on The Lord; and do well in a content manner in their current position.

All the while trusting God to make it happen that their effort is recognized by the necessary quarters and in His timing bring their desired promotion to fruition. God sees and knows the intent of your heart. The very thoughts you entertain; He sees and judges these by the intents. So do not think that you can hide anything from your Creator. He sees and knows it all! The more emotionally intelligent you are, the more self-evaluation you will do on a daily basis; If your thoughts are right as admonished in Philippians 4:8, you are less likely to embark on actions and behavior that is not pleasing to God. Let us have a closer look at the scripture.

"For the rest, brethren, whatever is true, whatever is worthy of reverence and is honorable and seemly, whatever is just, whatever is pure, whatever is lovely and lovable, whatever is kind and winsome and gracious, if there is any virtue and excellence, if there is anything worthy of praise, think on and weigh and take account of these things [fix your minds on them]. Philippians 4:8 (AMPC)

Since our language, actions and behavior follow on from the thoughts we have entertained and allowed to take hold the most in our conscious mind; it is important to be mindful and to be careful of the thoughts we entertain and dwell upon. So being mindful of our thoughts is key to keeping healthy thoughts in our minds. So look at the checklist carefully, are the thoughts true, arc thcy noblc, pure, lovely, of good report and even if they meet all the aforementioned, is there any virtue and are they praiseworthy?

Martin Luther King once said that **"you can't stop a bird flying overhead but you can stop it nesting in your hair"**. If the thoughts do not pass the litmus test above rid the mind of it and replace them with wholesome thoughts. How do I keep wholesome thoughts you may ask? Whole some thoughts are best for our minds, they are progressive and of virtue as well as are of praise worthy. So in the scenario earlier, walking in contentment and doing the job in your hands diligently while waiting on God is preferable.

Emotional Intelligence (EI) comes to play when we empathize with others and eventually do what we would expect to be done to us rather than consider only yourself as the rightful person to benefit in this scenario. Emotional Intelligence describes intrapersonal intelligence and interpersonal emotional intelligence. While the 'intra' EI addresses how much you are in tune with what is happening within you; the interpersonal EI relates to how much we are able to put ourselves in other peoples' shoes.

You need a good balance of both to have a robust personality! We shall see how a group of lepers demonstrated a healthy balance of emotional intelligence in the next scenario.

'Dare To Do It' Attitude

Embracing change is about daring to do it anyhow! At certain times in our lives, we reach crossroads where we think to ourselves, which way do I go? How do I get over this hurdle? Does it sound familiar? These are moments when no advice or help from anyone will do. I guess you have been at such points; I have certainly been there many times. These are the decision-making moments, when we are sure beyond doubt that our present state is not what or where we'd rather be, We create in our minds a favorable state (desired outcome) and weigh up options associated and then take the leap of faith. At that instance, we make a choice to embrace change by taking the plunge, in which we may either sink or swim to safety. Such is this story from 2 Kings 7:3-16 (NKJV):

There was great famine in the land of Samaria, such that people resorted to cannibalism (eating human flesh) to survive. In the scheme of the prophetic utterances of a greatly anointed prophet, Elisha, some remarkable events occurred. Now there were four lepers sitting outside the city gates who made a choice to dare do something about the problem shared by all. Of all the able-bodied men in the city of Samaria, it took these four leprous men to talk about their present state of hunger and desperation; even amidst their deplorable state of isolation and desolation. (A lesson to learn from these brave men, amidst adversity instead of pity party, they bounced ideas off one another)! They did not only stop at talking about their unfavorable situation, but actually dared to imagine an outcome if they were to do something. Let us look closely at the nature of the ailment these four men suffered.

Leprosy also called Hansen's disease (HD) is a chronic debilitating skin disease caused by the bacteria *Mycobacterium leprae* and *Mycobacterium lepromatosis*. Named after physician Gerhard Armauer Hansen, leprosy is primarily a disease of the peripheral nerves and lining of the upper airway; the disease produces skin lesions, which are the primary, and often times the obvious initial external sign. The ailment is impossible to hide; people see the lesions and if left untreated, leprosy can become progressive, causing permanent damage to the skin, nerves, limbs and eyes. Contrary to folklore, leprosy does not cause body parts to fall off, although extremities can become numb and/or diseased because of bacterial infection. With time, these extremities like the toes and fingers can loose nerve sensation; this infectious condition results in tissue loss, so fingers and toes become shortened and deformed as the cartilage is absorbed into the body.

Although the mode of transmission of Hansen's disease remains uncertain, most investigators think that M. leprae spreads from person to person in respiratory droplets. The period between which one comes in contact with the bacteria and manifestation of the first symptom called the incubation period is reported to be as long as 30 years, or over, as observed among war veterans known to have been exposed for short periods in endemic areas (areas where leprosy is commonly seen) but otherwise living in non-endemic areas. The minimum incubation period reported is as short as a few weeks, based on the evidence that leprosy has been reported among young infants born to sufferers. The average incubation period is between three and five years.

Leprosy is neither sexually transmitted nor highly infectious after treatment. Approximately 95% of the average population is naturally immune and sufferers are no longer infectious after as little as 2 weeks of treatment. However, I must add that this infection had no recognizable treatment during biblical times; so sufferers were placed outside of the community in colonies. They were ostracized from the healthy general population. Does that sound familiar, certain circumstances may make us seemingly ostracized from the people that we know and the people that we love. It is well, what is important is that we never ever give up on ourselves. We still have our minds that we can hook up to God, our maker, The One Person who never gives up on us. Friend, hook up to the God channel today.

Continuing with story: These four men had a disease that sentenced them to a lifelong of physical disabilities, social isolation, and emotional isolation too! They were totally ostracized from their own people, their society, they were outside the city gates according to the account in the Bible. Having leprosy had a huge stigma associated with it. I bet they had a fair share of being and feeling socially rejected too! Such feeling that is capable of creating very poor self-esteem within themselves and also being constantly undermined by others. Having the condition meant that the lepers can only find companionship amongst fellow lepers (does this sound familiar?). They were four of them who sat to carefully review their present state in relation to the mitigating circumstances shared by all in the larger society - the prevailing famine situation in their city. *"Why sit here until we die?" they asked each other. "We will starve if we stay here and we will starve if we go back into the city; so we might as well go out and surrender to the Syrian army. If they let us live, so much the better; but if they kill us, we would have died anyway."* - 2 Kings 7:3-4 (TLB).

Four desperate, desolate and diseased men realized they had nothing to lose. (Have you heard the saying that **desperate times call for desperate measures**? Just how desperate have you been lately?) Daring to face the unknown but trusting in the God who has answers only is the spirit of winners. Persevering until change comes true is the right attitude of winners and not of losers.

These men were dissatisfied with their present situation and they thought about options and talked about an action plan that had no guarantees! They sought some change. They may have been diseased in their physical bodies, however, their minds retained the capacity to evaluate their present state against an imagined state, which in itself did not hold out any guarantees of success. However, they dared to embrace change having weighed the situation they were in for any benefits or losses that may be associated with their options.

These men, even though they were unwanted for any social interaction by their own people and hunted by the enemy by the sounds of it, they had a hunch that sparked a glimmer of hope in their souls. "It's possible the Syrians won't kill us," they thought to themselves. "There is an outside chance they may feed us." What a lesson to learn from these dare-to-do-something leprous men!

When you think that you are facing an impossible situation, open your eyes and seek guidance of God. Dare to see the glimmer of hope that lies at the end stage of the change process. These men could have wallowed in self-pity, while moaning all day long as well as choose to be indifferent about their situation; after all they were going to die eventually anyway. No, they demonstrated a power-propelling attitude that is not common today. The power to evaluate their present situation in a realistic way, they took small achievable steps that edged them forward to where they desired to be. They had a high level of insight (self-awareness) and they chose to do something about their circumstances, not allowing fear to cripple them to inaction.

I recently heard a preacher, Mrs Ashimolowo, on National Television say this phrase: *"Great minds have and talk ideas, mediocre minds talk about events while small minds talk about other people".* How true indeed! These lepers had great minds irrespective of their physical and emotional disabilities. In this life, when situations that seem insurmountable threaten to drown you, make a choice to take the bulls by the horn, embrace change. Brainstorm for ideas and build on those ideas to bring dreams to reality through the change process. Dare to break the *status quo* and embrace the change process. Once you have an idea of where you wish to go, break this down into small achievable steps within a specific time scale. (*"Write the vision down and make it plain!"* - Habakkuk 2:2).

Do not settle for discouragement; neither settle for any less than you are purposed for. Arise from the pit of self-pity and discouragement, arise with confidence and spread your wings to fly to your glorious destiny.

However, I must state that firstly, you must be willing to embrace the process involved in between where you are and where you desire to be; the initial aspects to prepare for the change process; and commit all to God as advised in Proverbs 3:5-6 (AMPC)

"Lean on, trust in, and be confident in the Lord with all your heart and mind and do not rely on your own insight or understanding.

In all your ways know, recognize, and acknowledge Him, and He will direct and make straight and plain your paths."

Be obedient in the guidance and direction you get from God. Total obedience to follow as you are being led is crucial to achieving success - eating the good of the land. (Isaiah 1:19). These were the main characteristic qualities that made mere lepers become dare-to-do-it celebrities! They made a choice because they realized that they had the ability to respond in appropriate ways even in their desperate circumstances.

This particular story was one of success. This is not always the case in reality. Do not allow that in itself discourage you in anyway. Life is full of risks and only takers of risk are darers who often stretch to reach their desired states.

What do you have to lose if you follow that ray of hope anyway? It will lead you out of the spiritual, emotional and financial swamp in which you are stuck. Just dare to look within, look up to God, believing Him for that God factor and dare to take action on the dream of a more favorable desired state. Most importantly, dare to embrace the change process.

These lepers set out on their journey to the enemy's camp despite their disabilities. They were not going to allow anything dissuade them, step by step with trepidation, no guarantees assured at all and probably uncertainty sometimes loomed, they continued on their journey. Eventually they got to the camp (it is not recorded exactly how long the journey took them, however it can be deduced from the prophecy by the man of God, Prophet Elisha that it all happened within a twenty four hours period see verse 1,2 and verse 19 and 20) but can you just imagine, some of these men may have lost their big toes, which is very important in the act of walking and maintaining balance; but still they launched out for the camp of the Syrian army, the enemy's territory with their vision strong and alive! Isn't it interesting that when the mind is focused on a mission, the body moves along with such speed? The lepers journeyed into the camp of the Syrians.

The account continues (in verse 5) by a step of dogged faith, casting aside every fear, they arose beyond their fears and doubts and arrived at the camp of the Syrians. By the providential hand of God, some other event was happening possibly at the same time the lepers were contemplating to set off to the Syrian camp. The story describes what ordinarily we would call coincidence in the 21st century; however, it did happen by the divine orchestration of God's hand; and the lepers found that the Syrians had fled from their camp leaving behind all their wealth and possession intact.

The lepers arrived at the camp, at to their utmost

surprise, they saw much more provisions than they could ever have imagined. These lepers hit the jackpot! Great abundance of food, wealth and indeed plenty of resources compared to the famine they have become used to lately. This is what happens when we dare to believe and exercise faith in the God who is more than enough. God always exceeds our expectations! Note the word **"expectations"**. We must have the expectations in the first instance. He gives us more than we can ever imagine or think; always, God exceeds our expectations! His great provision meets every need even when we do not have any idea how. Let hope arise within you at this moment. This may be the only moment you will ever have to seize the opportunity. Believe God is able to bring about change in any and every situation in Jesus' name. Amen.

(I want you to imagine in your mind's eye that you were one of such persons suddenly walking into plenty and surplus after experiencing an intense period of famine or lack).

It was time for them to eat and enjoy their newfound wealth! How would you fare if you are faced with a similar situation? I ask myself. These four men carefully sat to eat as much as they could and started to pick as much silver, gold and clothing as they could. Then suddenly started to question their actions and the fact they have been silent about their discovery of plenty. These lepers had a way of exercising their thinking ability, choosing to exercise their ability to respond appropriately in situations. They stopped to reflect and evaluate their actions and their thoughts yet again in that moment (putting themselves in the shoes of others – interpersonal EI). Can you imagine what their thoughts, feelings and actions could be at that very moment in time? This is a unique characteristic of great minds and highly effective people, they stop to think, reflect, evaluate and make necessary changes, the spontaneity and adjustment, Wow!

These lepers remembered their city and the state of impoverishment that prevailed for many others! Rather noble of them. Yes, I say noble because these were men whom the society did not reckon to be a part of them anyway. They were at the city gates, ostracized from the general population. They could have been morally justified to keep the secret of sudden wealth and newfound status and just enjoy this. All four, deliberated and decided to return to inform the King's household.

The moral of this story:

Irrespective of the peculiar nature of your circumstances, God is not bound by time or geographical distance: *"We are assured and know that [God being a partner in their labor] all things work together and are [fitting into a plan] for good to and for those who love God and are called according to [His] design and purpose."* (Romans 8:28 AMPC)

God is able to make ALL things (the good, the bad, and the ugly) to work together for your good because you love Him, and you are called according to His purpose.

Given all circumstances, God is and remains a CONSTANT in the equation of my life. You can work with this mathematical equation of life too irrespective of the adversity or situation. If you make God, The Holy Spirit and the Word of God as the ultimate term of reference and at the centre of all that is in your life, then this becomes a good base to work out all other variables of life.

Irrespective of the area of life that calls for this change, there is the need to start by creating in your mind your desired outcome, evaluate your present situation and weigh up the associated benefits with options available to you.

Firstly, the initial stage starts with thinking in a productive manner. You need to understand the 'eyes' through which you view your life and the outer world; and explore how you can alter this viewing 'eyes' to that of your Creator, God. Ask yourself, how does God see the peculiar situation of mine? Take more than one perceptual positions to enable you have a fuller picture.

Look into The Bible, find relevant scriptures that will help you formulate the desired goal. Anchor your prayers and petitions around these scriptures.

MindWorkout Gym Exercise:

I encourage that you attempt to do this exercise.

1. Get an exercise notebook and a pen.

2. Close your eyes in a quiet room with little distractions. Quieten your mind and allow your mind to be blank for a moment. How hard is it to do this? Put a percentage rating to this. Date it and note it down. Begin to feel the love of God as you stay your mind on God (Isaiah 26:3) - "You will keep him in perfect peace, whose mind is stayed on You"

3. *Aim to tune your spirit to The Spirit of God. Enjoy Gods peace, and oneness in yourself.*

4. *Now try to imagine that you are watching: your own funeral and you see your body lying there motionless, see in your mind's eyes all your loved ones, and well-wishers holding a notepad to write a thing or two about you when you were alive.*

5. *Write down what you imagine these people will be writing down about you. (Remember that you are doing this through other people's 'eyes')*

6. *Carefully take particular note of what your spouse and children will have to say of you.*

7. *Then your close friends and extended family; and then your work colleagues and so on include your enemies if you have any or many.*

8. *At this moment step back into your living self and write down what you think these categories of people in your life may have had to say in your notebook.*

9. *How did you find that experience? Write it down truthfully in your special notebook.*

This exercise is useful in many ways. It helps you visualize the end and how you would wish it to be remembered – desired outcome. It also enables you to evaluate in an objective way, how you view yourself and your world in the now. As well as enabling you have a goal to start working towards.

If you know your desired outcome, then you know how

to research and prepare to achieve this. Try compiling your information in a table as shown on the next page.

Your willingness to be open minded and some degree of will power are the most common ways of influencing a change in any aspect of life. Habits are formed when consistently practiced in about twenty-eight days approximately according to psychologists. Simple activities such as keeping a reflective journal on a daily basis over a period of month can produce the work of self-evaluation. Having identified certain behaviors, you want to change, consider application of sound, colour and depth to these, and given time, this process of change will slowly but surely happen.

Take home message:

'In this life, when situations that seem insurmountable threaten to drown you, make a choice to take the bulls by the horn, by embracing change the God way. Brainstorm for ideas and build on those ideas. Conscientiously work to bring the dream to reality through the change process. Dare to break the status quo and embrace the change process. Once you have an idea of where you wish to go, break this down into small achievable steps within a specific time scale'. Take action, and do it with guidance from Gods word, The Holy Spirit and prayers in Jesus name.

Category of persons	Spouse		Children		Close friends		Acquaintances		Extended family		Your enemies	What values /attributes you wish to see the most (list)	What do you need to start doing (list)
	How you see it now	How you desire	How you see it now	How you desire	How you see it now	How you desire	How you see it now	How you desire	How you see it now	How you desire	How you see it now	How you desire	

Chapter 5

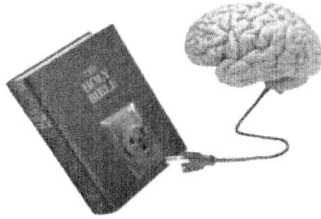

Perception and Perception Shifting

We are creatures of a truly great God; saved by the blood of Jesus Christ and we can choose to live our lives to please Him, to do His will, and to fill the earth with His goodness. One good way to bring about change is to shift our perception on situations. The simple act of total submission of our will to God prepares us for what we are created to do - to worship God by doing His purpose for making us in the first instance! Jesus Christ came to the earth to do the will of God - the Father; and indeed He completed His task in an excellent manner. This was pleasing before God and today Jesus sits in the heavens at the right hand of the Father having earned this prestigious honor through OBEDIENCE!

According to Neurolinguistics Programming (NLP), the results you create in the process of change in any area of your life are caused by what you do and especially your external behavior. Because your behavior is influenced by your thoughts, feelings and emotions as well as your perception of reality it is your responsibility to embrace change that can make you achieve your desired outcomes. Choosing to learn small but effective steps in the change process on a daily basis, you can significantly improve your results in whatever area of life.

Perception, simply put, is becoming aware of our environment/reality through our senses. In other words, perception is a way of interpreting physical sensation in the light of our unique life experiences. Due to this fact, perception is inherently connected to consciousness, awareness, comprehension and cognition. The five representational systems invariably are our senses (sight-Visual; hearing-Auditory; feeling-Kinesthetic and the taste and smell-Olfactory).

Every human being's perception differs at any point in time principally because of the particular mode of perception that we employ. Our capacity to comprehend any percept (stimuli) is determined by the number of senses we have involved in the perception process and the systems by which it makes meaning to us. It is the state of the mind that matters.

To further drive this home, four people may be viewing an object and yet have four or more ways to represent what they are seeing. The choice of words to describe the object, the depth, angle and even previous memories of similar or same object; all go to influence how each person views this object and thus also determines how their brain interprets what each person believes is before them.

Perceptual Filters

In NLP, the belief is that as humans, in comparison to animals, filtering external stimuli/information via our sense organs occurs by three main processes: by deletion, distortion and by generalization; otherwise we would be completely overwhelmed by the information overload through our senses. Thus our senses perceive through some filters in the whole process of experiencing everyday reality around us. Animals, on the other hand, have specialized perception ability that adapts them to their environment. For example, bats and dogs are able to hear certain sound frequencies that humans cannot.

Using Perceptual Positions as a Modality of Change

John Grinder (1987), one of the founders of NLP formulated perceptual positions as operational extensions of the earlier NLP concepts of 'referential index' (words that identify the persons or objects to which a particular statement is made), meta positions (a.k.a. meta model processes, one of which is the referential index shift technique involves a linguistic shift in which one pronoun was exchanged for another) and Gregory Bateson's concept of 'double' and 'triple' description.

An example of referential index shift is explained below as given by Bandler and Grinder:

"My husband doesn't appreciate me.....My husband never smiles at me." In order to shift the referential index, the therapist will ask the client, "Does your not smiling at your husband always mean that you don't appreciate him?"

Jesus Christ used similar language patterns in His time on earth. It is a powerful linguistic tool to make people deeply reflect upon generalized statements and as such shift their perspective on an issue. There are other 'meta positions' which act as a strategy for resolving inner conflict. 'Meta' position involves establishing a perspective 'above' and 'between' contradictory internal parts or 'polarities' according to Grinder and Bandler, in the structure of Magic volume 11 (1976).

An example of a 'meta' position was demonstrated by Jesus when He was before Caiaphas, the high priest just before His crucifixion. In Matthew 26:62 Jesus demonstrated a Meta position with respect to the polarities of the situation before Him. Jesus had choices about action/behavioral options. There was uncertainty in the mind of the high priest about whether Jesus will behave in a way that is characteristic of one polarity or the other. However Jesus, in a smooth and coordinated fashion, appropriately and congruently communicated both polarities in a way that expressed either polarities appropriately. Jesus was God in that He is part of the trinity. He was equally human and Caiaphas asked Him a question: "I put You under oath by the living God: tell us if You are the Christ, the Son of God." Jesus did not need to be put under an oath for a truthful confession even though He, on numerous and different situations, had indicated His divine nature and unity with the Father. Jesus' reply was brilliant and exquisitely put "*It is as you said, Nevertheless, I say to you, hereafter you will see the Son of Man* (referring to his human self) *sitting at the right hand of the Father, and coming on the clouds of heaven.*"

Meta positions involve more than a simple combination of the polarities or parts in conflict. They point out that if a client has two polarities (A and B), Meta position would be some representation (C) that had "all the potentials of A and B as well as Not solely A and Not solely B; instead the rich choices that results from the many combinations within and between the polarities". As an analogy, rather than turn 'black' and 'white' into 'gray', meta positions allows the use of black and white to make complex and beautiful patterns.

In relationship difficulties, the use of Meta positions is helpful in management of conflicts. For instance, in an interaction between a husband and a wife, if either were to use a Meta position, this will involve such one to dissociate (take oneself out of that conversation loop) him/herself from the interaction and reflect on one's own behavior within the relationship to the other. Meta position puts such a one temporarily out of the communication loop to gather information about self and the other party as though he was a witness to, and not an active participant in the communication loop. In this position, the individual can see, hear and feel what the interaction conflict truly is through the eyes of a 'witness' interested but very much a neutral observer.

An instance in my very turbulent marriage, when I in a reflective and one of a few quiet moments, asked my ex this question;

"If I was your sister and I came to you as my elder brother to explain all the experiences I have had within this marriage, would you think your sister has had a fair deal?"

To which he replied "No".

Bearing in mind that this was a marriage characterized with physical, emotional and psychological abuse. My ex, prior to then, was always very defensive of the happenings and as such we had huge difficulty at resolving our conflicts. I remember telling him that, for once, I have heard him respond in a sincere and truthful manner. My next question was "why then do you put me through this?" By this time, our marriage was at a stage of significant disrepair; there were no redeemable elements; the marriage eventually ended in a divorce a few years later. The point of emphasis is that in a Meta position, conflicts can be resolved because at least one of them is willing to take the 'interested impartial onlookers' position. A lot of insight can be acquired that will hopefully assist the change process within the relationship.

I explored this as one of the ways to help identify certain problematic areas in our reality in the present; as well as explore potential solutions also.

Chapter 6

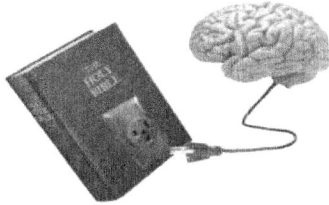

Cell-To-Cell Communication

C ell to cell communication, also known as Cellular communication, is an umbrella term used in biology and more in depth in biophysics, biochemistry and biosemiotics to identify different types of communication methods between living tissues.

The human body is complex in creation as well as in understanding too! However, we do know that just as the human being exists as spirit, soul and body, so also every cell in the body has the ability to exist and interact with one another. The processes by which this communication happens can be neurological, electrical and chemically as well as spiritually (believe it or not!). Every cell in our bodies has the qualities of a living entity. These are then intricately organized within unique organ systems. So within the organ the cells have a communication style and within organs, there is also a wider communication system too.

Human knowledge is limited; however, science describes some of the methods of communication to include cell signaling among others. This process allows millions of cells to communicate and work together to perform important bodily processes that are necessary for survival. Both multicellular and unicellular organisms heavily rely on cell-to-cell communication.

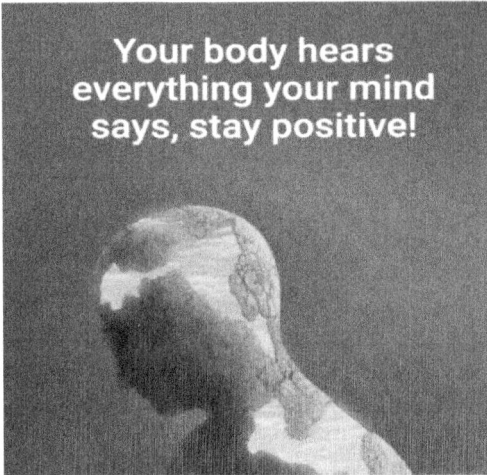

Your body hears everything your mind says, stay positive!

All cells receive and respond to signals from their surroundings. This is accomplished by a variety of signal molecules that are secreted or expressed on the surface of one cell and bind to a receptor expressed by the other cells, thereby integrating and coordinating the function of the many individual cells that make up organisms. Each cell is programmed to respond to specific signals outside the cell (extracellular) to other molecules. Extracellular signalling usually entails the following steps:

1. Synthesis and release of the signalling molecule by the signalling cell;

2. Transport of the signal to the target cell;

3. Binding of the signal by a specific receptor leading to its activation;

4. Initiation of signal-transduction pathways.

Cells have receptors which can bind, respond to signals via chemicals and electrical impulses according to what message is received.

I do not wish to bore you with the intricacies of cell-to-cell communication but suffice to mention that cells in our bodies can hear, respond, speak to one another and translate messages in complex manner one to another. So if your ears hear words like, "I'm doomed", the message is transmitted to all other cells to prepare for what is being communicated. Likewise, if the message is "I am alive, alert and enthusiastic", the cells in your ear organ will transmit or cascade this accordingly for all the other cells in your body to respond. Isn't that incredible? Little wonder the scriptures describe King David as saying in Psalm 19:14 (ESV) *"Let the words of my mouth and the meditation of my heart be acceptable in your sight, O Lord, my Rock and my Redeemer."*

"Set a guard, O Lord, over my mouth; keep watch over the door of my lips!" - Psalm 141:3 (ESV)

"I tell you, on the day of judgement people will give account for every careless word they speak." - Matthew 12:36 (ESV)

"Death and life are in the power of the tongue, and those who love it will eat of its fruits." - Proverbs 18:21

Since God's Words never return until they have accomplished what it was sent forth to do (Isaiah 55:11) and we were made to be like Him, our words have creative ability also.

If salvation can come by confessing Jesus as Lord, how do you think even other words you speak cannot create, destroy or bring about a change? So as James admonishes us in James 1:19, "let us be quick to hear, slow to speak, slow to anger".

The relevance of this in embracing change is this:

Experiments have been done, even though disputed by the scientific world, relating to certain aspects of this assertion – that cells of plants have the ability to respond to the emotions in humans. A man called Cleve Backster, who worked for many years as a CIA agent in the USA, described intent, attunement and spontaneity as very essential to the attainment of positive outcomes in his experiments. Many new age religions use some aspects of these phenomena in certain healing practices.

As children of the Most High God, I know that our words have power to effect change in circumstances and they also have an impact on our emotional states. The more you speak positive words of affirmation to yourself, the more positive emotions and emotional states you have. The contrary is true, the more negative words you speak and listen to, the more negative emotional states you experience.

Thinking that we only exist in the physical is a fallacy! Just as God exists as Father, Son and Holy Spirit, so also we exist as spirit, soul and body. Our body was made from the earth so it returns there at death. The human spirit is the breath of God. As long as we have the breath, we are alive; however, at death, the spirit returns to the Maker; since it is the breath of God that makes us living souls (Genesis 2:7 KJV). The soul is the sum of your personality, your mind with all the emotions, will, memory, intellect etc.

Every cell in our bodies has this composition in order for harmonious co-existence within ourselves as well as to interact with our environments. Anatomy teaches us that the complex and intricate mechanisms of the respiratory and circulatory systems of the body ensures that oxygen carried by special blood cells reach every cell to bring nourishment and similar systems take away wastes products from the cells to the right organs, the Kidneys, largely to rid the body of such. All the bodily systems work in harmony so we are in health and thus are able to function properly. The ultimate purpose of this harmonious and systematic existence of all the cells in the body is to be able to, in a coherent manner, bring glory to God by performing the work(s) of the Living God here on earth.

Whatever we think about and speak out has profound impact on how the cells of our bodies react and also on how the environment responds too.

At the beginning of this book, I mentioned how God created us in His likeness and in His image. God made us to be like Him in every way; to be able to create and alter our states, our bodies and our environments by relying on His resources - prominently His Word and His Spirit. The more of God's Word that informs your thoughts, the more your words also will be influenced by scriptures. Surely, this is a winning combination! Your thoughts and your words aligning with Gods Word brings us in right standing with God and thus brings us favour with God, favour with men and most of all health to all of our flesh.

<u>MindWorkout Gym Exercise</u>*:*

Knowing that our cells hear and respond to what we say, how do you intend to speak more wholesome words?

What do you need to do?

We need to think carefully of our words even when we are angry; words spoken cannot be retrieved.

Some are in the habit of using a phrase like this "I'm afraid ...." Unknowingly such persons are communicating fear to all their cells little wonder they become fearful and nervous wrecks in their personal lives.

Personally, I speak with confidence and boldness because the scriptures tell me that I have not been given a spirit of fear; but of power and of love, and of a sound mind. (2 Timothy 1:7; Isaiah 50:4 NKJV)

Monitor your language over the coming four weeks and identify areas of disempowering language use and change these to align with Gods Word.

I recommend a book called <u>"30 Days To Taming Your Tongue"</u> by Deborah Smith Peques.

Chapter 7

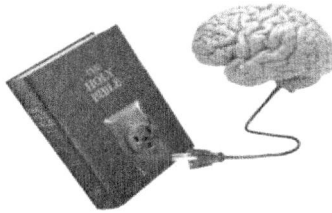

Understanding the 'How's of Mental Health Disorders

The 'eyes' through which we view the world affects our emotions, feelings, attitudes and behaviour. That is why our peculiar circumstances, experiences and exposures make us exactly how we are today. In examining how we may end up with mental health disorders (often referred to as aetiology), there are certain factors that interact in a complex manner to produce how a mental disorder display itself in the present.

Categories	Psychological	Biological	Social	Spiritual
Predisposing	Upbringing environment	Genetic;	Parenting style Use of peculiar language patterns	Lack of use of principles of faith
Precipitating	Prolonged and perceived stressors/threats Lack of healthy coping skills Personality type	Perceived stress; Use of mind altering substances e.g. cannabis, cocaine and even alcohol excessively etc. Use of prescribed medication such as B blockers (propranolol) or steroids Chemical imbalances occurring in the brain from protracted exposure to adverse situations	Adverse e.g. housing; financial	Inadequate or lack of and in depth knowledge of faith principles
Perpetuating	Ongoing stressors and not seeking appropriate help Unhealthy attitudes Personality type	Ongoing perceived stressors	Lack of job satisfaction Use of unhelpful coping strategies	Both of the above and not seeking to address this

The above aetiology grid is an attempt to explain how various factors may interact in a complex manner thus result in predisposing, precipitating, or even perpetuating mental disorders.

The genetic predisposition describes the inherent vulnerabilities that we are born with for instance, the illnesses (physical as well as psychological) that our close family members e.g. parents suffered with which may have been passed on in our genetic makeup. By way of genetic inheritance as well as style of upbringing (parenting) we are exposed to in childhood, our personality is slowly but surely formed. Being exposed to praise and open communication in an environment where love is expressed openly tends to result in a generally healthier personality type.

Exposure to excessive negative criticisms, bullying, suspicion and belief in ungodly practices and explanations of such as reason why adverse situations happen tends to result in a personality type that is paranoid, defensive and often unwilling to accept responsibility for personal development and the need for change. Does that sound familiar? I bet you can think of one or two persons with such personality types.

While there is no one single personality type that is better than the other, being balanced in approaches to managing change and stressful situations of life is key to having an okay-ish personality.

The column on Spirituality is one of increasing recognition within the World Health Organization and the

Royal College of Psychiatrists. The role of spirituality in the aetiology, manifestation as well as in the management of mental disorders. There is a Spirituality Special Interest group within the Royal College of Psychiatrists in the UK and there is a growing presence of chaplains and imams on psychiatric units to help resolve some complex issues regarding the interface between mental health disorders and patients spiritual beliefs. There is also a growing use of mindfulness and meditation as interventions on the ward and patients find the relevance and benefits in their recovery pathway.

In a survey done a few years back now in which patients were asked what spirituality meant to them, the following were interesting responses as recorded on the Royal College of Psychiatrists.

People with mental health problems have said among others that they wish to have the chance to make sense of their life – including illness and loss as well as have the permission /support to develop their relationship with God or the Absolute. In response to this and other initiatives, it is more accepting in the UK, for someone with a religious belief to be offered some of the following

- a time, a place and privacy in which to pray and worship

- the chance to explore spiritual concerns

- to be reassured that the psychiatrist will respect their faith

- encouragement to deepen their faith

- (Sometimes) to be helped with forgiveness.

The major problem which faces the National Health Service has been the poor embrace of this culture across board. There is no consensus on how spirituality concerns of patients must be addressed; current practices vary from region to region and on the s p e c i f i c   n e e d s   o f t h e   patient and where they are at on their recovery journey.

However, patient–carer groups and other stake holders continue to lobby for spiritual needs of patients to be acknowledged and facilitated. Health workers often shy away from discussing spirituality needs of patients either because they lack the expertise or they fear the repercussions that have been mentioned in certain quarters. Exploring spirituality is very relevant either in the perception, acceptance of the mental disorder or even in the recovery phase. In my clinical practice, I often recommend sessions with a chaplain in situations where I perceive a patient stands to benefit. In my local church, I am able to explore more the interphase between my career and my faith much more. I have offered open CBT groups to members of the congregation to explore the common mental disorders and the use of scriptures in sustaining the benefits of the therapy - CBT.

Habits Can Grow To More Problematic Habits

Certain unhealthy habits formed during our childhood and adolescent years can trigger the onset or the worsening of existing mental disorders on the short term and long-term basis. For example, out of wishing to belong or to be accepted in a subculture, young persons may start smoking cigarettes. By this simply innocuous habit formed, they become more likely to smoking cannabis, a mind-altering substance. May I use this opportunity to highlight certain concerns known of Cannabis.

Role of Psychoactive Substances

Psychoactive substances are mind-altering substances, which can cause chemical imbalances in the body. Statistics show that 1 in 4 persons use psychoactive substances for recreational purposes. Since this book may not be able to explore all psychoactive substances, I shall only discuss Cannabis and its effects.

Cannabis a.k.a. marijuana (sometimes spelled "marihuana") among many other names, is a derivative of *cannabis sativa* - a naturally occurring plant. According to the United Nations, cannabis "is the most widely used illicit substance in the world." It is estimated that over 192million people aged 15 to 64years habitually use Cannabis. Repeatedly, research studies have identified heavy and continuous use of Cannabis can trigger onset of major psychotic disorders as well as negatively affect the prognosis of existing psychotic disorder. Cannabis is a psychoactive drug. I have huge and growing concerns about the future of the young generation of users, as we are likely to have a future of adult cannabis users with significant recurring mental health problems - if latest research evidence is anything to go by.

There are about 400 chemical compounds in an average cannabis plant. The four main compounds are called *delta-9-tetrahydrocannabinol (delta-9-THC)*, *cannabidiol,delta-8-tetrahydrocannabinol* and *cannabinol.* Apart from cannabidiol (CBD), these compounds are psychoactive, the strongest one being delta-9-tetrahydrocannabinol. The stronger varieties of the plant contain little cannabidiol (CBD), whilst the delta-9-THC content is a lot higher.

In more recent times, there have been synthetic and adulterated Cannabis which are more potent and with worse consequences when used by persons already susceptible to developing mental disorders by way of their genetic vulnerability.

When cannabis is smoked, its compounds rapidly enter the bloodstream and are transported directly to the brain and other parts of the body. The feeling of being 'stoned' or 'high' is caused mainly by the delta-9-THC binding to cannabinoid receptors in the brain. A receptor is a site on a brain cell where certain substances can stick or "bind" for a while to exert some effect. If this happens, the cannabinoid exerts its effect on the nerve cell thus altering the nerve impulses it produces. Curiously, there are also cannabis- like substances produced naturally by the brain itself – known as *endocannabinoids*. These exist in small quantities and the body is able to rid itself of it after it has completed its designed effect.

Most of these receptors are found in the parts of the brain that influence pleasure, memory, thought, concentration, sensory and time perception. Cannabis compounds can also affect the eyes, the ears, the lining of the lungs, the skin and the stomach.

Cannabis has a peculiar poignant smell and it occurs in various preparations. Its usefulness has been known since as long ago as the third millennium BC. In modern times, the drug has been used for recreational, religious or spiritual, and even medicinal purposes. In 2004, the United Nations estimated about 4% of the world's adult population (162 million people) use cannabis annually, and of this population of users, about 0.6% (22.5 million) use it on a daily basis. These figures have increased astronomically worldwide since then. The possession, use, or sale of cannabis preparations containing psychoactive cannabinoids became illegal in most parts of the world in the early 20th century. Since then, some countries have intensified the enforcement of cannabis prohibition, while others have reduced it.

Despite the policy any Government adopts, some people still engage in profiting from the growing and marketing of Cannabis plant. It is a growing concern in the developed and the developing world as there is an upsurge in the growing use of this substance among very young persons. (The major concern being the more lasting structural as well as chemical changes imprinted on the growing brains). In the developing countries, the tropical weather enhances and flourishes its growth and ready availability. By way of cultural acceptance, younger children are getting exposed to its use. Research has shown that the effects of cannabis is dependent on the nature of what is used (whether synthetic or potent specie) used, the entire duration and consistency of use.

What Are Its Effects?

Some of the immediate pleasurable effects of habitual cannabis use include an initial relaxing effect; other physical effects include sleepiness; redness of the white of eye; increased ravenous appetite and a general calming effect. This often also leads to an exaggerated sense of omnipotence because of its mind altering capacity. It can also make colours brighter and more intense and music sounding better. Many artistic people who use the substance also claim that they are more inclined to be "creative" after using Cannabis. There could also be perceptual abnormalities which thus feeds into the suspiciousness and paranoia that is commonly associated with prolonged use.

Around 1 in 10 cannabis users have unpleasant experiences, including acute onset of confusion, hallucinations (perceiving impulses through their senses in the absence of stimuli), intense anxiety and paranoia – the belief that others are out to get or harm them. The same person may have either pleasant or unpleasant effects depending on their mood and circumstances. These feelings are usually only transient; although the drug can stay in the system for weeks to months because of its ability to attach to adipose fat tissue; the effect can be longer lasting than users realize. Long-term use can have a depressant effect, reducing motivational levels and in severe cases cause a syndrome called "amotivational syndrome". This condition is characterized by a wish not to engage in any positively stimulating or goal directed mental activity eg studying. This directly explains why young scholars tend to drift from their academic work and start to attain very poorly before eventually dropping out of the educational system.

The longer term effects as demonstrated from very robust longitudinal research has shown that over time a form of tolerance (a psychological situation whereby increasing amount of the substance is used with time to produce the initial effect) occurs with prolonged and heavy use. There could also be withdrawal features if there is an apparent reduction in the level of use (these can include intense craving for Cannabis, thus seeking to use Cannabis against all sensible activities and by any means.

Anthony et al 2006, describes the lifetime risk of dependence among adult recreational cannabis users to be around 9%, rising to one in six among those who initiate use in adolescence.

Cannabis use disorder emerges with habitual use of cannabis within ten years. Amongst these are Dependence being one of the commonest complication and this is usually commoner in males as against female users and early age of exposure to Cannabis is a common denominator in both sexes.

The World Health Organization (1969) define drug dependence as a state, psychic and sometimes physical, resulting from taking a drug, characterized by behavioral and other responses that always include a compulsion to take a drug on a continuous or periodic basis in order to experience its psychic effects, and sometimes to avoid the discomfort of its absence. A syndrome (i.e. collection of signs and symptoms) commonly associated with cannabis use is a psychological dependence; prominently there is loss of control with intense compulsion to use cannabis against all rational explanations. A form of psychological dependence occurs with heavy and prolonged use, which is driven, by a need to ameliorate the adverse bodily effects brought on by not taking cannabis.

The typical Cannabis user over years of continued use becomes increasingly paranoid and suspicious of other peoples' actions because of their tendency to misinterpret normal perceptions and actions of others. In more severe cases, frank psychosis in the form of hallucinations: auditory (hearing voices when there is no one about), tactile hallucinations (experiencing sensations in their body when there is no actual stimuli) and can become thought-disordered (situations where the individual is unable to think clearly as well as unable to express their thoughts clearly in spoken or written language).

I term this stage as that of 'mash mellow brain stage' - when the brains substance struggles to perform simple everyday rational action sequences. As I mentioned earlier, cannabis just like any other mind altering psychoactive substance have the capacity to damage the cyto-structural (i.e. the architecture) and the chemical environment of the brain of its user. Reversal of these changes to normal may or may not happen. And even in total abstinence, there is often no guarantee of a return to full normal intellectual capacity.

This has huge consequences for young persons are students studying in College or University. Cannabis can interfere with attention and information processing ability of the brain. And as such it may interfere with a person's capacity to focus their attention or use information in purposeful manner. A large study in New Zealand followed up 1265 children for 25 years. It found that cannabis use in adolescence was linked to poor school performance, but that there was no direct connection between the two. It looked as though it was simply because cannabis use encouraged a way of life that didn't help with schoolwork.

Let us explore the effects on a person's ability to function effectively and efficiently at their occupation. Cannabis seems to have a similar effect on people at work. Even though research evidence did not establish a direct causal relationship between non-achievement and cannabis-use, observational studies have established associations that are compelling. Most users are more likely to leave work without permission, experience proprioceptive and poor coordination of their dextral abilities; spend work time on personal matters or simply daydream. Cannabis users themselves report that drug-use has interfered with their work and social lives. This effect is attributable to its effect on judgement and complex decision-making ability of the frontal lobe areas of the brain.

Of course, some areas of work are more demanding than others. I am sure you will not wish a dentist or a surgeon who habitually uses cannabis to perform surgery in your body or in a family member's!

A review of the research on the effect of cannabis on pilots revealed that those who had used cannabis made far more mistakes, both major and minor, than when they had not smoked cannabis. As you can imagine, the pilots were tested in flight simulators, not actually flying. The worst effects were in the first four hours after cannabis use, although these mistakes persisted for at least 24 hours thereafter, even when the pilot had no sense at all of being 'high'. The study concluded, "Most of us, with this evidence, would not want to fly with a pilot who had smoked cannabis within the last day or so" according to information from the Royal College of Psychiatrists. UK.

Cannabis and its effects on driving?

In New Zealand, researchers found that those who smoked Cannabis regularly, and had smoked before driving, were more likely to be involved in a car crash. A recent study in France looked at over 10,000 drivers who were involved in fatal car crashes. Even when the influence of alcohol was taken into account, cannabis users were more than twice as likely to have caused a road traffic crash by their judgement errors. In addition, it was found that these crashes were more than likely to be fatal than other crashes. So by extrapolation, perhaps most of us would also not want to be driven by somebody who had smoked cannabis in the last day or so. However, how can we tell what drug-taking habits drivers of commuter vehicles have in the developing world? I guess until there are better ways of detecting this, we all need take the responsibility for our safety. If you can, get to see the driver of any vehicle you intend to travel in, have a light-humoured conversation with him to ascertain for yourself whether you are able to pick on one or more of the physical effects described earlier.

Mental Health Problems Attributable To Cannabis Use

There is growing evidence that people with serious mental illness, including depression and psychosis, are more likely to use cannabis or have used it for long periods of time in the past. Regular and habitual use of the drug has appeared to double the risk of developing a psychotic episode or long-term schizophrenia. However, there are few questions we may ask at this juncture; such as: does cannabis cause depression and schizophrenia or do people with these disorders use it as a self-prescribed medication to cope with the symptoms they may be experiencing?

Over the past few years, research has strongly suggested that there is a clear link between early cannabis use and later mental health problems in those with a genetic vulnerability and that there is a particular inherent risk with the persistent or heavy habitual use of cannabis by adolescents.

1. Depression

A study following 1600 Australian school-children, aged 14 to 15 for seven years, found that while children who use cannabis regularly have a significantly higher risk of depression, the opposite was not the case. Children who already suffered from depression were not more likely than anyone else to use cannabis. However, adolescents who used cannabis daily were five times more likely to develop depression and anxiety in later life.

2. Schizophrenia

Three major studies followed large numbers of people over several years, and showed that those people who use cannabis have a higher than average risk of developing schizophrenia. If you start smoking cannabis before the age of 15, you are 4 times more likely to develop a psychotic disorder by the time you are 26. They found no evidence of self-medication. It seemed that, the more cannabis someone used, the more likely they were to develop symptoms of a psychotic disorder (severe mental condition in which there is marked blurring between reality and fantasy; there may be abnormalities evident in the speech, thinking and behavior patterns of sufferers; typically there is a complete disorderliness and lack of rational and logical socially appropriate behavior taking into consideration age, cultural and societal status).

Why should teenagers be particularly vulnerable to adverse effects associated with the use of cannabis? No one knows for certain, but it may be something to do with effect of cannabis on brain development. The brain is still developing in the teenage years – up to the age of around 20, in fact. A massive process of 'neural pruning' is going on. This is rather like streamlining a tangled jumble of circuits so they can work more effectively. Any experience, or substance, that affects this process has the potential to produce long-term psychological effects including psychosis as well as cognitive functioning.

Recent research in Europe, and in the UK, has suggested that people who have a family background of mental illness and so probably have a genetic vulnerability anyway, are more likely to develop schizophrenia if they use cannabis.

Is There Such a Thing as 'Cannabis Psychosis'?

Recent research in Denmark suggests that yes, there is Cannabis Psychosis - just like any other psychoactive has the ability to cause a condition termed 'substance induced psychotic disorder'.

Cannabis Psychosis is a short-lived psychotic episode that seems to be triggered by cannabis use but which subsides quickly if the individual has stopped using it. It is quite unusual though that in the whole of Denmark they found only around 100 new cases of new onset psychosis with cannabis use per year was observed.

However, they also found that:

- Three quarters of habitual cannabis users had a different psychotic disorder diagnosed within the next year.

- Nearly half still developed a psychotic disorder over the 3 years that followed.

It seems probable that nearly half of those diagnosed as having cannabis psychosis are actually showing the first signs of a more long-lasting psychotic disorder, such as schizophrenia. It may be that this group of people are particularly vulnerable to the effects of cannabis, and so should probably avoid it in the future.

In early 2011, travelled to Nigeria and I was terrified by the use of cannabis openly on streets of Lagos by very young people. Can you see where my concerns are coming from? The possibility of mental health problems of these young people in the future!

Cannabis and Addiction:

Is cannabis addictive? Cannabis has some of the features of addictive drugs such as:

- Tolerance - having to take more and more to get the initial effect

- Withdrawal symptoms - shown in heavy users and include craving, decreased appetite, sleep difficulties, weight loss, aggression and/or anger, irritability, restlessness, and strange dreams.

These symptoms of withdrawal produce about the same amount of discomfort as withdrawal from tobacco or alcohol.

- For regular, long-term users: 3 out of 4 experience cravings; have become irritable

- 7 out of 10 switch to tobacco in an attempt to stay off cannabis.

- The irritability, anxiety and problems with sleeping usually appear 10 hours after the last joint, and peak at around one week after the last use of the drug.

Compulsive use: The users feel they have to have it and spend much of their life seeking, buying and using it.

They cannot stop even when other important parts of their life (family, school, work) suffer.

Physical health problems: The main risk to physical health from cannabis is probably from the tobacco that is often smoked with cannabis. As such, similar risks of mouth, throat and lung cancers associated with smoking cigarettes is associated with cannabis use.

It is safe to assume that prolonged and heavy use of cannabis is a recognized cause of major psychiatric disorders like schizophrenia especially in people who have existing genetic susceptibility to develop mental illness.

There is also a social drift of these individuals because of the decline in intellectual capability to cope with demanding mental tasks.

There is so much to say about cannabis but let us return to the subject at hand: how aetiological factors interact in a complex manner to result in mental disorder.

In the management of mental disorders, the approach again is as it is with the aetiology. Approaches used in the treatment of mental disorders fall within one or more of the following:

- **Biological approaches**: these include the use of pharmacological (medication/drugs), physical (Electroconvulsive Therapy, ECT)

- **Psychological approaches**: various forms of talking therapies – IPT (Individual psychotherapy), CBT (Cognitive Behavioural Therapy) and Psychoanalytical psychotherapy.

- **Family therapy** in cases of young persons with addiction problems.

- **Social approaches**: psychosocial interventions; long term supportive psychotherapy.

- **Spiritual approaches**: use of scriptures in mindfulness and CBT delivery styles as in MindWorkout Gym approaches.

Chapter 8

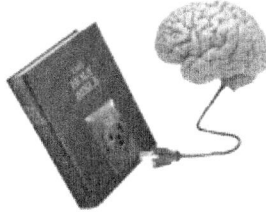

Maximizing the Mind

The mind and how it works is already fascinating; but when the scriptures also ask the questions below, then my imagination goes into hyper-drive.

- Where is the mind anatomically-situated in the body?

- Physiologically, how does it function?

- What is the mind about? What exactly is it?

- Why is it, that even the greatest palm reader; or psychic could not access a man's mind except there is cooperation from the subject?

It is truly great that we have the power to guard our minds (allow or stop anything into our minds). The mind may not be a tangible organ in the human body; however, it exists and it is the window to the true self (man).

Theologians and Philosophers have varied and

inconclusive evidence to support its existence. This is a great thing in itself, because there are many other people who have been curious too! You and I know that there is an aspect of a human called the mind; and this may be described as the seat of the intellect and its soundness determines how mentally stable we are. Fair description I would think but the fact is that it exists and has great potential.

As a practicing Christian, I choose to explore this topic from a biblical perspective. I get excited when I think of the fact that we were made after the true likeness of a Creator with a Great Mind.

The inward man is virtually synonymous with the mind and it finds delight in the law of God. This delight causes Christian believers to want to align themselves with the new nature God promises to impart to them. There are many scriptures in the Old Testament which refer to the fact man is unable to have access to God's wisdom in his own strength. Equally, there are New Testament scriptures which describe a process of daily renewing the mind with the Word of God and the Psalms corroborates with Hebrews 4:12 in saying that God searches the intents of the mind. Spiritual transformation starts in the mind!

A renewed mind tends to think soberly of oneself; a crucial step to behavioral change is self-observation. If we agree on the point that the mind is the seat of cognition in the human, then we can deduce that our actions, feelings and behaviors are a consistent way to make a guess as to what is happening in an individual's mind. Some agree and others do not concur that every human being has a 'free will' to make choices. Irrespective of that, your choices speak volumes to others in the society as to what may be taking place in your mind.

I have always known that our senses (hearing, sight, smell, tactile as well as the 'eyes' - perceptions we choose) are windows to this unique entity called the 'mind' and that the most senses that you predominantly operate in determines which modality you are most operational.

Your tendency to speak or view life through certain modalities makes you operational as follows: Thoughtful people tend to consider issues and they tend to speak using a preference for words like 'I think' or 'I believe'. Those who are more auditory will use terms like 'I hear'; the visually operational tend to use terms like 'I see' in their descriptions and those who are emotive predominantly will use terms like 'I feel'. The importance of knowing which modality we are more operational helps with self-discovery. In the absence of knowing and understanding yourself, there is total chaos and you do not have a predetermined mode of operation. I shall liken the latter group to the 'tumbleweed mind'. Anything goes! There is no filtering, no redefinition and no characterization of all the information entering the mind through the windows of the mind - your senses.

MindWorkout Gym Exercise:

Over the next few weeks, think of which group you may belong. This can be done by just pausing to question your actions, thoughts and feelings even more importantly your choice of words in spoken or written language. It could be a painful exercise but it is extremely useful in enabling you to know yourself better.

Self-discovery is the first step in self-actualization. As you discover yourself, you will gravitate towards self-development to be the best that you can be.

Available Therapies mental health disorders:

A) Biological therapies include use of various medications as deemed by specific patient characteristics, choices, guided by the treating physician.

 Electroconvulsive therapy and psychotropic medication use. There are different classes of psychotropic medication: - Antidepressants; Antipsychotics; Anxiolytics; and Antiepileptics etc.

B) Psychosocial interventions, supportive therapies

C) Psychological therapies e.g. Cognitive Behavioural Therapy (CBT)

D) Spirituality: emphasis on use of scriptures for Christians

E) Other forms such as Art therapy, creative therapies such as music therapy and other biblio therapies/ interventions

Concerning various bio-psychosocial interventions for mental disorders, the National Institute for Health and Clinical Excellence (NICE), an independent organization in the United Kingdom, has been charged with the responsibility of providing national guidance on promoting good health and preventing and treating ill health.

In practicing psychiatry for almost three decades, I have seen first-hand, the effectiveness of biological and psychological interventions such as Individual psychotherapy, group psychological interventions. More importantly, research has proven the efficacy of CBT (Cognitive Behavioural Therapy) in prevention, treatment of disorders such as anxiety, depression and other psychological problems. CBT, simply put, is an intervention, which helps people to be more aware of their thinking and how this influences their feelings, emotions and behaviours.

Practicing mindfulness is equally extremely effective in the management of common situations of anxiety, self-esteem, and distress associated with unforgiveness. Various mental disorders affect our intellectual ability and everyday functioning. Stretching this further, exploring the spiritual dimension is equally important. There are ongoing studies that are exploring the relationship between spirituality and mental disorders.

Thoughts tend to occur at three levels: Thoughts, Assumptions and Core beliefs. The scriptures can have profound influence at each level; however, the persistent use over time may be far more applicable at the level of core beliefs. Negative thought patterns (NATs) that emerge from core beliefs are often more difficult to overcome, however, use of affirmations with ongoing perseverance with the new method of self-management brings relief with time.

The scriptures refer to part of the Fruit of the Spirit (Galatians 5:22-23) as being 'self-control' - which can be defined as an act of mastering one's emotions rather than to be controlled by them. Behavioural and cognitive approaches within the Vygotskian framework, describes integration with a range of options that enable clients to become experts in self-regulation of their own behaviour. From my background in Learning Disabilities, I am mindful that in Applied Behavioural Analysis, (ABA), the key concepts of self-regulation and self-motivation tied in with the cognitive elements makes a beautiful way to help clients connect the complexities between cognition and language use. Self-control within ABA perspective is the giving of reinforcers to oneself and presupposes that the individual client has the inherent ability to 'obtain reinforcement but fails to do so until a particular response has been emitted' (Skinner, 1953, pp237-238).

Activities like self-monitoring by recording one's behaviour, self-evaluation by rating one's behaviour against a criterion, in this instance, the scriptures; and self-reinforcement (affirmation with scriptures) are key processes in achieving any desired outcomes. Mastering one's emotions in this way is an empowered state that the client becomes an agent of control over his or her body-thoughts, behaviour and language. This thus suggests the heightened level of self-understanding by way of self-awareness and self-discovery; attributes equally implicitly encouraged in CBT.

Other scriptures, which share CBT tenets, refer to healing power of scriptures over mental and physical health problems alike.

Proverbs 4:20-22 (NKJV) *"My son, give attention to my words; Incline your ear to my sayings. {21} Do not let them depart from your eyes; Keep them in the midst of your* heart; {22} *For they are life to those who find them, and health to all their flesh"."*

Proverbs 3:8 (NKJV) *"… It will be health to your flesh, and strength to your bones".*

Exodus 15:26 (NKJV) *"… I am the Lord who heals you".*

1 Peter 2:24 (NKJV) *"… by whose stripes ye were healed."*

Psalms 107:20 (NKJV) *"… He sent His word and healed them, and delivered them from their destructions."*

Isaiah 53:5 (NKJV) *"He was wounded for our transgressions, He was bruised for our iniquities; the chastisement for our peace was upon Him, and by His stripes we are healed"*

If the mind is the origin of our thoughts, then an effective way to tackle Negative Automatic Thoughts (NATs) will presuppose a gradual transformational change.

The Framework for CBT

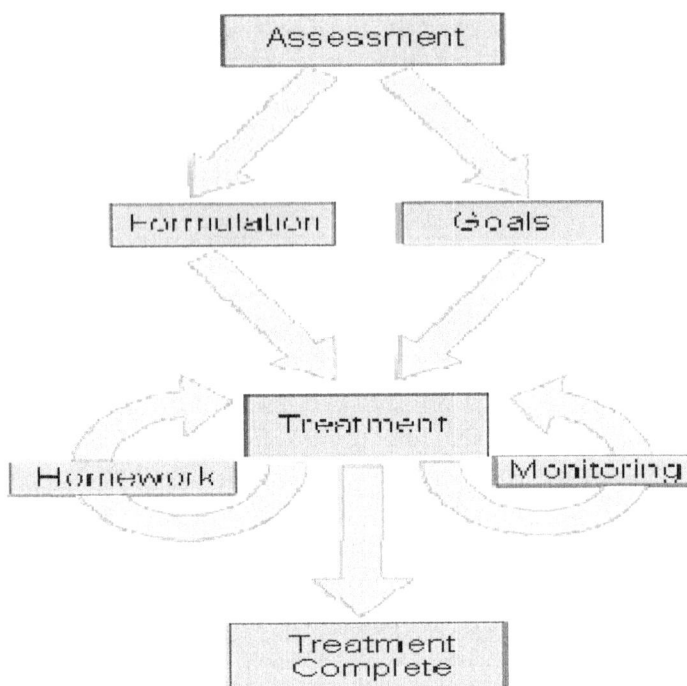

Figure.1

The goal in CBT is to break the vicious cycle linking NATs with unhealthy feelings and emotions; thus empowering the patients to experience relief.

At assessment stages:

- Identify the problem areas themselves; quantify the degree of distress associated with the problem in a written formulation.

- Identify and link the components of the problem-thought, feeling, emotion and behaviours (actions/bodily reactions) involved.

- Identify the goals they wish to achieve, assist them to formulate a strategy which breaks the desired goal into smaller achievable steps so that at each stage the patient can quantify the distress level they wish to experience so that when it happens they are able to appreciate progress made.

The client is enabled to view his/her problem from an objective position, so s/he take ownership in the entire process from assessment to treatment.

The client is encouraged to focus at what is happening on the inside in the here and now and the relevance to the specific problem in question during the week as part of the homework. By so doing, the client engages in guided discovery and self-monitoring; this helps increase an awareness of the body processes like thoughts/feelings/body reactions/ and resulting behaviour.

The MindWorkout Gym

Embracing change by engaging the scriptures is the very basis for the MindWorkout Gym. Most people spend hours in the gym working out or scheduled weekly exercises; the physical body becomes stronger, fitter and more toned. This outcome does not come about after only one day of workout but from a habitual lifestyle of regular exercise. There are other benefits from physical workout; endorphin release results in good feelings and improved mood. The process of joining a gym or just jogging in the open can also bring about some social connection benefits. More importantly, all of these address some aspects of the human condition- the body and by inference, the mind.

The thinking behind the MindWorkout Gym (MWG) is to develop the habitual workout of staying (fixing) our minds on scriptures (Isaiah 26:3). From earlier discussions, we have agreed that the BIBLE is the Basic Instructions Before Leaving Earth. Our spirit is the aspect of a human being which has the ability to connect with the Spirit of God. Doing the workout via the modality of the MWG fills our minds with what is the perfect will of God (The Word of God is food to the spirit of man as physical food is to the body). It is popularly stated that you are what you eat! Likewise, you are spiritually alive, alert and growing by the transformation and renewal of your mind through the revelation knowledge of the Word of God you have believed and have applied in your daily living. It is in so doing that we live intentionally and purposefully.

We are able to think more like our Maker! If you and I know more about God's Word (that has the dynamic ability to bring the whole world into being as well as sustain it); assimilate and apply the Word in everyday living, then our lives becomes transformed in a way that enables us to enjoy life rather than to simply exist. By habitually meditating on the word of God, we extract the nourishment that grows our spirits need to mature with time. Filling our spirits with the Word brings us on the path of living for God's glory – the ultimate plan and purpose of man. (I have run workshops on the Mind Workout Gym as well as have a Facebook presence on MWG).

Chapter 9

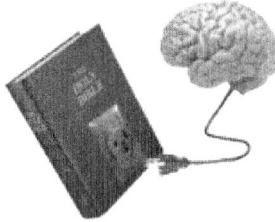

Healing and Spirituality

The healing process not only has a tendency to bring people closer to an appreciation of who they are as individuals, it also brings them closer to God while creating a sense of calm in their inner person, spirit, ushering inner peace, connectedness, or whatever we choose to call that which is great and mysterious. The longer I have considered this fact, the fundamental connection between healing and psychological wellbeing, the more I think of it as one of the most remarkable signatory details left to us by the Architect of human consciousness – God Almighty Himself.

Consider how truly elegant the design process is that created us so that in the face of the most difficult times of our lives, there is the possibility, not the certainty but the possibility of an access to states of awareness and experience that enable us to cope with these crises better than we otherwise would. Spiritually, there is growing evidence from various research activities in the USA & UK to support the notion that one's spirituality influences aetiology as well as the process of healing of physical as well as mental disorders.

Religion and spirituality are among the most important cultural factors that give purpose and meaning to human values, behaviours, and experiences. Spirituality is derived from a Latin word – *spiritualitas*, meaning "breath". It can be very personal with an experiential element to it. Personally, I believe spirituality is the yearning arising from deep within a human for a sense of connection with a supernatural being that can bring a sense of completeness, self-integration and often a sense of wholeness. This lends itself to the notion that there is a 'void' in humans and the personal search to fill this void is embodied in activities termed 'spirituality'. This aspect that often influences our core beliefs and views of the outer world and ourselves. This concept lies within every human. The very sense of 'an integrated-self' lies deep within the meaning of spirituality. Connecting with one's spirituality gives a sense of meaning and purpose to life. Religion, on the other hand, can be perceived as the culturally-acceptable way of expressing this yearning within a group who share similar beliefs.

Most of the major religious groups do share the concept of spirituality albeit with some permutations. Spirituality brings about inner healing due to the sense of self-acceptance and integration of the whole self, spirit, soul and body as well as the reliance on the transcendence of connectedness to a higher being.

Studies suggest that addressing patients' spiritual needs facilitates recovery from illness. Some studies in the United States of America compared the treatment of depressed religious persons with standard CBT with religious content and with pastoral care alone revealed that the latter group had significantly less post treatment depressive symptoms compared with the group who received standard CBT. Deductions from these studies support the notion that spiritual beliefs held by people have intrinsic and complex influences on their patterns of coping as well as their overall sense of wellbeing; and that spiritually-augmented CBT may have therapeutic benefit in people of faith suffering from depression. The observable benefits included rapid recovery and less symptomatology months to years following therapy. Studies that are more recent offer consistent result findings with this observation.

Lovett (1985, p.33) stressed the importance of self-determination especially through a collaborative relationship between the therapist and the client. With this comes a therapeutic alliance; an aspect that has been shown by studies to be a powerful tool to enhancing therapy outcomes.

In collaboration with a colleague of mine, we decided to conduct a pilot study titled Mind Workout Gym early in 2010. The results of that pilot study was consistent with previous research findings that habitual use of scriptures help sustain the benefits of CBT.

Is There Any Healing In The Word of God?

Healing can be psychological, emotional, as well as physical and even spiritual too. We shall dwell hugely on psychological healing in this book as we have already talked about mental health disorders.

The Word of God is contained and derived from the Scriptures (BIBLE). The Holy Scripture describes an act of transformation of the mind by daily renewing of the mind with scriptures. The Bible teaches Christians a stepwise way to follow for managing everyday anxieties. The Holy Bible is key in enabling Christians enjoy peace as a part of their daily life (Philippians 4:6 (NKJV)) - if they accept to first believe and allow the practice of word study, meditation in stepwise approach as directed. There is an element of choice, which is important to the success of CBT even in non-Christians. Pure CBT, as against CBT using scriptures, prescribes use of more positive and healthy thoughts as alternative options for NATs. In this, I find loose and possibly a contributory reason why benefits from conventional CBT are not sustained over time. Scriptures tend to be specific and have the inherent ability to effect change even at a molecular level in the life of a Christian. The emphasis here being in exerting a choice to apply scriptures in situations suggests this construct of self-mastery while depending on the transcending power of the Holy Spirit[1] to help, teach and guide in the process.

In Luke chapter 4:18-19, Jesus read from the book of Isaiah saying *"The Spirit of the Lord is upon me, because*

---

[1] The Holy Spirit is not a vague, ethereal shadow, nor an impersonal force. He is a person equal in every way with God the Father and God the Son. He is considered to be the third member of the Godhead with a clear role to help, teach, guide and bring believers to all truth. John 14: 16-18 (NKJV)

he hath anointed me to preach the gospel to the poor; he hath sent me to heal the broken-hearted, to preach deliverance to the captives, and recovering of sight to the blind, to set at liberty them that are bruised, to preach the acceptable year of the Lord."

The ministry of Jesus, when He was on this earth, included the healing of various kinds of sicknesses and diseases including broken hearts. Jesus was not a physically trained physician; however, he was the greatest of Physician that existed. Indeed He is the Healer. There was miraculous healing works in His words, His touch and even on the hem of His garment. The scriptures record that people got their healing from even the gaze and walking through the shadow of His followers. As it happened in those days, even so testimonies abound in the present day across the world. Just as belief and Faith in Gods' word and ability (Hebrews 11:1, 6) is an important ingredient to the process, so is forgiveness (Luke11:4).

The word "broken-hearted" refers to how we can be hurt or broken in our mind - thoughts, feelings or emotions rather than the break of the anatomical heart. It means the circumstances and events of life that can hurt us and shatter the wholeness of our spirits. Our minds can be broken by any memory where there is emotional pain or negative emotions. Our minds are broken in situations marked with loss; this is experienced and sometimes interpreted as pain, anger, resentment, hatred, unforgiveness or bitterness. The human mind can also become broken at the remembrance of any such memories where there is perceived shame, guilt, regret or sorrow.

The scriptures have provision for every manner of healing and that includes means by which our broken hearts/mind can be mended. Not only our broken hearts but also a lot of our physical or mental health problems as well. Whether we want to believe this or not, negative emotions emanate from our perceptions most of the time and these negative emotions can cause physical and mental health problems if we do not deal with them in a timely manner. We do not have to live in the bondage of negative emotions. Jesus has provided a way by which we can be healed from our past or present negative emotions and even in the future. For in Jesus Christ all things consist (hold together); and that includes our healing.

Jesus' manner of healing is found in the principles of repentance, forgiveness and letting go of hurt. When we choose to forgive those who have hurt us in any way, the anger, hatred, resentment and bitterness is removed. The heaviness of the hurt and pain lifts from our hearts. Our choices in everyday events are crucial here! The fact is that we can choose to forgive what is happening today and purpose to forgive even what will happen tomorrow and in the future.

Repentance will free you from all the shame, guilt, regret, and sorrow in your memories. When we repent, Jesus is faithful to cleanse us. When He forgives, He completely and utterly forgets about our sins. The scriptures describe this that *"as far as East is from the West, that's how God has removed our sin from us"* (Psalm 103:12, CEB). If He can do this for us despite all our shameful acts, how come then we cannot forgive the hurt from other people? If we look to and ask God for mercy, then we ought to also graciously offer mercy to others as well. For when we show and demonstrate forgiveness to others, we release ourselves from the associated pain. We also bring ourselves to the position whereby we can receive our healing from God.

In famous scripture known as The Lord's Prayer in (Matthew 6:12, 14-15 CEB) *"Forgive us for the ways we have wronged you, just as we also forgive those who have wronged us. If you forgive others their sins, your heavenly Father will also forgive you. But if you don't forgive others, neither will your Father forgive your sins".* It is well stated that we get forgiveness from God for our sins as we forgive others who sin against us. Forgiveness sets you free from the bondage of the pain. It does not only set the person who hurt you free but it releases YOU, (the person who has been hurt) from the associated pain. Everyone will answer to God for their sins. God is just and fair, and every act of omission or commission of sin will be judged only by God We cannot sit in the place of judgement.

The scriptures make it clear that when we choose not to forgive others, then it makes it doubtful if we will ever experience the forgiveness of our own sins by God. To forgive others is a choice we have to make.

If you need that healing, should there be any pain that is so great that you cannot let go?

Is your healing not worth much more than that resentment, hurt or pain caused you?

By the stripes of Jesus' wounds we are healed so is recorded in Psalm 103:3 and 1st Peter 2:24 as well as by prophet Isaiah 53:5. However, you must first accept God's grace (unmerited favour) for salvation. Jesus declared on the cross of Calvary "It is finished" no matter what your diagnosis is. The King of all ages says "it is finished" to your illnesses or diseases. Accept the finished work of Jesus, believe this deep in your heart and confess this and be healed. Allow His Word to influence the change process in every aspect of your life.

(Matthew 19:26 CEB) says *"its impossible for human beings. But all things are possible for God".*

Healing In Reconciliation

Jesus taught that the law is summed in these two:

"Thou shall love the Lord thy God with all thy heart, strength and thy entire mind; and thou shall love thy neighbor as thyself." - Matthew 22:37-39.

MindWorkout Gym Exercise:

The point of full reconciliation with God, yourself and others is the point where your healing begins. So in the coming weeks and months, consciously decide to be in a position of full reconciliation with everyone as you start your change process. It is a major requirement before you can start your healing journey. Walking in unforgiveness and not letting go of hurt prevents the free flow of God's blessing healing into our lives; particularly in the area of healing which is part of our blessings to enjoy!

I was pondering on this scripture recently and these thoughts flooded my mind, which I believe I could share here. Psalm 1:1-3 (CEB) says:

"The truly happy person doesn't follow wicked advice, doesn't stand on the road of sinners, and doesn't sit with the disrespectful. Instead of doing those things, these persons love the LORD's instruction, and they recite Gods instruction day and night! They are like a tree replanted by streams of water, which bears fruit at just the right time and whose leaves don't fade. Whatever they do succeeds. That's not true for the wicked! They are like dust that the wind blows away. And that's why the wicked will have no standing in the court of justice - neither will sinners in the assembly of the righteous. The LORD is intimately acquainted with the way of the righteous, but the way of the wicked is destroyed."

The NKJV version of the same scripture puts it this way:

"Blessed is the man, who walks not in the counsel of the ungodly,
Nor stands in the path of sinners, Nor sits in the seat of the scornful;
But His delight is in the law of the LORD, And in His law he meditates day and night.
He shall be like a tree Planted by the rivers of water,
That brings forth its fruit in its season, Whose leaf also shall not wither;
And whatsoever he does shall prosper."

Have you ever wondered after you have been through some tough situations in life and say "Boy, just how did I survive that period of my life? How did I pull through? Where did I find the strength to go through that?".

There is a way for the righteous and the wicked; clear pathway and rightly so is their end also. There is an end that is justified for them who are diligent in their walk with God and in whom is their delight.

Mindworkout Gym Exercise:

- *Are you planted by the waterside?*

- *What do you need to do to fit the profile of the righteous described in this passage of scripture?*

- *Where do you find your strength and pleasure?*

- *Are your roots deep and leaves ever green to survive the drought? How can you habitually bring this to happen in your everyday life?*

The drought comes in many times and assuredly will test every aspect of your life. Your feelings will fail you sometimes; your situational/momentary reasoning will challenge your beliefs and all you have ever heard of the Word of God. Be planted in the house of God even when you do not feel like it. When you face some 'hellish' experiences, as you may well know, it could be a lonely time when you are often on your own. The key to surviving is tapping survival resources from fellowship with God and from God's Word. Those lonesome moments may, however, sometimes be good to a certain extent.

The tests you are going through right now are trying the Word of God that you have in you - if you are a believer. We are admonished in the scriptures that *"having done all to stand"*. It is on Christ, the solid rock, alone that I can stand; all other ground is sinking sand.

The cares of life can beat you down and wear you out if you do not have the deep roots in fellowship with God. The deceitfulness of riches may also distract you. Remember you need to seek the Kingdom of God and its righteousness first, and all these things will be added unto you. (Matt 6:33 AMP) *"But first and most importantly seek (aim at, strive after) His kingdom and His righteousness [His way of doing and being right – the attitude and character of God], and all these things will be given to you also".*

God is a jealous God; be careful that the cares of this world do not distract you from following Him. If you pursue success in the absence of God and His righteousness, then you could run the risk of worldly suffocation!

It is a choice that you must make like Paul did. As for me, I will not allow anything to separate me from the love of God.

- Are there issues competing for your attention at this moment?

- Are there near choking experiences? How can you use scriptures to stay afloat?

- How terrifying can this be?

Physically-speaking, during episodes of choking, you fear that you may lose your life if you do not do anything about this. This is the same way it is when life's problems come our way. The choice is yours. Hold onto success at all cost and run the risk of dying spiritually as well as physically. You've got to dislodge the cause of the obstruction (whatever is choking you) so that you can enjoy the goodness of God! Stand firm and hold unto God's Word (Proverbs 4:20-22). God's Word has life and has the proven remedy to sustain you in whatever season of life.

You may ask "but how can I be planted by the waters?" By developing a process of connecting in your thoughts to God, (Isaiah 26:3). Seeking to dwell in the presence of God, you get connected by faith to the God of the entire universe. The fruit of His righteousness which includes joy, peace, favour, abundance on this earth and all the goodness of God will be your portion. Seek God's face in prayers and the revelation knowledge in God's Word.

Many times after turmoil comes the breakthrough (marked with joy and brightness of day). When God is ready to connect you to your breakthrough, He will do the entire breakdown that is needed to bring you to your peculiar designed life path. He will strip down all the distractions until you are bare! You must be willing to stay put. After the trying (drought) periods, then you are refined and ready for that breakthrough that only God has the power to do as He wishes, just rejoice and be available. When you do your part of the business, God turns everything that has been negative, around for your good. He will see, acknowledge and recognize you in your corner. Be strong and grow roots that are deep and dependable.

In the times of trials, the depth of your roots will see you through the valleys and peaks of all your drought moments in this change process. Personally, I have come to know that regularly practicing a simple act of shutting off my mind to all distractions in the environment enables my mind to focus and connect with the presence of God[32]. It could be seen as a form of mindfulness/meditation but it is such a useful way of quietening my mind, shift perspectives and focus on the important matters in life. This exercise is refreshing and very rewarding in interrupting the vicious cycle of NATs during CBT. When a human has a grip on the purpose of being, then that being will have a sense of a secure base or anchor. Wholeness to a person is more about their understanding of themselves and how they fit in the greater picture, rather than just being complete individual within oneself. When this happens, life makes sense, because we see life outside of ourselves and in the now of what the scriptures say specifically. Thus, we see our now as a point on a timeline of purpose and we see ourselves as another link in the chain connecting one significant event to another.[3]

It suddenly sinks in that we are all vulnerable! There is no exception! The Office of National Statistics (ONS) UK states that 1 in 4 people will develop a form of mental disorder in their lifetime. The truth is this: a diagnosis of mental illness can lead to a profound transformation of values just like the diagnosis of terminal illnesses like cancer. Things that used to seem important often become less salient, while other values to which you may have given little thought take priority. This sorting process can go on throughout one's life. Choices are made based on information and sometimes on intuition.

---

[2] Holy Bible (NKJV). Isaiah 26:3 *"Thou will keep in perfect peace whose mind is stayed on Thee because he trusts in Thee."*

[3] Holy Bible (NKJV) Acts 17:28 *"For in Him I live, move and have my being"*

While a cure is a successful medical treatment, it can be seen as a treatment that removes all evidence of the disease and allows the person who previously had, for instance, cancer to live for as long as he would have lived without cancer. A cure is what the physician hopes to bring to the patient.

In the treatment of mental disorders, cure is more of a rarity. The relapsing nature of most mental disorders makes the process of healing far more acceptable.

Healing, in contrast to cure, is an inner process through which a person becomes whole; healing can take place at the physical level, as when a wound or broken bone heals. It can take place at an emotional level, as when we recover from terrible childhood traumas or from the pain of the death of a loved one or a loss as in a divorce. It can take place at a mental or cognitive level, as when we learn to reframe or restructure destructive ideas about ourselves. This is the level at which choices hugely play a role. We could choose to get on with our lives (in effect 'enjoy' life) irrespective of what has happened to us or carry the burden of resentment and anger. It can take place at what some would call a spiritual level, a much higher level of healing as when we move towards God, toward a deeper connection with nature, or toward inner peace resulting from a greater sense of connectedness.

For any cure to work, the physical healing power of the organism need be sufficient to enable recovery to take place. Likewise the healing in a variety of mental disorders involves the conscious and deliberate effort by a patient to rise above past trauma and wrong doings and forge ahead. This in itself does not rule out the need to see a professional if your symptoms are severe to impair your day-to-day living. When in doubt seek to see a qualified professional for appropriate help.

When a physician sets a bone or prescribes an antibiotic for an infection, he is doing his part for recovery by offering curative therapy. Yet, when the inner healing power of the organism is insufficiently strong, the bone will not set or the infection will not subside. Healing is thus a necessary part of being cured – a fact with profound implications for medicine, since the authentically holistic physician is deeply aware of the essential role his patient's recuperative powers play and will do everything he can to encourage the patient to enhance those recuperative powers including their spiritual beliefs.

One's spiritual beliefs has the potent power to keep hope for the present and the future!

Clinical Vignette:

46-year-old, AG, is a single non-practicing, Church of England, Christian. The Caucasian female presents with history of recent onset episode of very disruptive behaviour (chasing an acquaintance around with a knife because she has a belief that this lady is the female who made a fleeting encounter she had on a cruise in her twenties come to an end). She is arrested and undergoing Police investigation. She is one of three children, born to dysfunctional family unit. Her mother was an alcoholic and heavy substance user (opiates, cocaine and cannabis), who sadly died recently. Patient was abused sexually by her elder brother for years till adolescent years.

Disclosure of this fragmented the family. Father moved away and remarried. He suffered with severe Depression with some experience of hearing voices when no one was present. He died three years ago.

AG lacks any depth of emotional connection to her family. Had a few intimate relationships and ended recently diagnosed with HIV. She is open to meet with the chaplain because of the intense guilt she is experiencing. She had in the past carried out acts of self-harm including an attempted suicide. She was fortunately found by a neighbour after taking an overdose of all her medication 6 weeks ago.

Could this lady, AG be suffering with a mental disorder? If yes, of what nature is this?

And why is this lady presenting with this at this point in time?

An attempt to understand the interactions between the aetiological factors in the above vignette; let us fill the grid below:

	Predisposing factors	Precipitating factors	Perpetuating factors
Biological factors e.g. genetic predisposition.			
Psychological factors e.g. early upbringing, coping skills			

Social factors: environmental exposures, live in plenty resource-wise			
Spiritual exposures: e.g. how grounded was she in her belief in God and His word? How much is his everyday life being governed by God's word?			

MindWorkout Gym Exercise:

Were you able to identify all the biological/psychological/social/spiritual factors which may have predisposed, precipitated or even perpetuated this presentation above?

Can you confidently fill many boxes above with the scanty information in the vignette? Evidently whatever presentation needs to be quantified in the light of how much this is affecting their everyday functioning of all within the family unit.

What is the severity of the mental disorder?

Is there any impairment of everyday functioning?

Does the duration of symptom presentation meet the DSM-IV (Diagnostic and Statistical Manual, 4th edition) or ICD-10 (International Classification of Diseases, 10th edition)?

These are the international diagnostic manuals by which diagnoses are made worldwide. They both help to standardize as well as maintain research integrity.

Details of your attempt at filling the grid and any questions can come be sent to me via email: admin@edge2balanceliving.com

Chapter 10

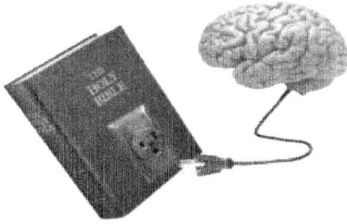

The Secret of Trying and Not Giving Up

The Secret of Trying and Not Giving Up

Have you ever wondered why it feels like everyone else seem to be succeeding with little effort and it feels you are just stuck and not moving quite at a meaningful pace like them? It is a common experience to us all.

Life is ever evolving and people are in dynamic motion flowing along. Some are making the most of opportunities to become successful while others are not. I once met a man who gave me an acronym P.O.O.R - standing for People Overlooking Opportunities Repeatedly are the POOR. That is so true indeed.

Are you overlooking opportunities that come your way repeatedly? Alternatively, do you belong to the category of people who do not even see the so-called opportunities because you are so preoccupied? Look up and pray that God will enable you see the opportunities He brings on your path. He gives you the ability to embrace whatever change that is needed to make the most of your life.

We are unique and each one of us is running a set race. We are not racing against anyone else but ourselves. As we put in our best trying to succeed at whatever we find to do, we must bear in mind that we are not in a competition with any other person.

In reality though, despite all our good intentions and hard work, it sometimes feels as if certain forces beyond our immediate control are forever moving the goal posts; this can be very discouraging. We can become fearful to try again or in extreme cases, we give up altogether! These are grounds to consider a famous saying that **winners don't quit and quitters don't win.**

Make a choice to be a winner and have a winner's mind-set – giving up is no longer an option!

If and when you find yourself at the point where you do not feel you need to try anymore, then you have walked yourself into a state of 'learned helplessness'. At this stage, you would have succeeded in learning and conditioning your mind that you are 'helpless'. Who says that you are? Even when the situation dictates that, get up and tell yourself that you can unlearn that process and keep on trying. You can make good things happen no matter the situation. You have all that it takes to make change happen inside you! You can do it.

Firstly, choose to learn lessons from the failed attempts so that you are thoroughly equipped with what it will take to have your breakthrough in the future attempts. Do you know how much is encoded in the human brain every waking second? If you had an idea, you would know that we are a peculiar race, tough, rugged and capable of effecting change by processes (learning and unlearning; associating and dissociating etc.). Perseverance and making the right choices does pay, keep doing it!

Consider this quote from the twenty-sixth American President:

"It is not the critic who counts; not the man who points out how the strong man stumbles, or where the doer of deeds could have done them better. The credit belongs to the man who is actually in the arena, whose face is marred by dust and sweat and blood, who strives valiantly; who errs and comes short again and again; because there is not effort without error and shortcomings; but who does actually strive to do the deed; who knows the great enthusiasm, the great devotion, who spends himself in a worthy cause, who at the best knows in the end the triumph of high achievement and who at the worst, if he fails, at least he fails while daring greatly; and his place shall never be with those cold and timid souls who know neither victory nor defeat."

- Theodore Roosevelt (1858-1919)

Even though we have many attempts at trying and success is not yet in sight, we need to persevere. This could be very hard indeed but remember it is not how far but how well rounded one turns out at the end. If we persevered at trying there is a greater probability that we shall triumph at the end.

Secondly, we need to be careful not to enter the competitive mind-set where we could become overwhelmed by envy and jealousy of others we perceive are succeeding. Offer genuine and sincere help to others when they need it. In doing so, great and multiple streams of blessing will open to you. Believe me, there is triumph with trying. This may take many attempts and more importantly perseverance but in the end we will surely triumph if we do not give up trying!

When nothing else will do ... just pray in this manner:

Father, I come to You just as I am without a plea but only upon the finished work of Jesus Christ. I come boldly to seek your face today. Honour and praise to You for this provision Lord!

I stand amazed at the wonders of all Your works all around me every day, thank you Lord! Knowing that as I seek you, You'll reveal yourself more and more to me, I say thank You! You guide my path and order my steps by Your Holy Spirit and Your Word, I say thank You Lord! The more I seek to know You the more You reveal yourself to me, I say thank You. Lord, give me the quizzing mind of a child always and may I never have enough of You all my days. Give me a meek and a contrite heart to learn from Your Word and know every prompt and leading lesson from the Holy Spirit, Amen.

Lord, each day You teach me a new lesson, may I always have a humble heart that is teachable. That I may be a fountain of physical, material and spiritual blessing to others, Lord this is my heart's desire. Knowing, Lord, that for me to be an effective tool in Your hand I need to position myself in You; deeply rooted and grounded in Your word, such that my will becomes enthralled completely in Yours. Once my will becomes Yours in every way, I'm fully ready to be a battle-axe in Your hands, Father, hear my prayers, Amen.

The fact that I can call You Father gives me a warm feeling inside; knowing that You accept me unconditionally, Lord I thank You. I long for deep revelation and knowledge of Your Word through Jesus Christ, the Author and Finisher of my faith. Truly You have taught me things in the past, Lord, today I hunger for fresh and new things from Your Spirit. Fill me and quench my thirst, oh God, in Jesus name, Amen.

Keep this hunger going Lord that I will always know that without You I am lost and cannot find my way through this life. I wish to be able to say honestly that I live each new day in a surrendered state of mind. A state of careless abandonment to Your will my Creator and my Maker. It makes me feel safe knowing that You are in total control of my life. I am relieved to know that every time I surrender to You and follow Your ways, You give me a new perspective on every situation. Lord, may my expectation not be cut off as I hope in You alone.

Thinking back, it breaks my heart how I have had so many shortcomings in meeting Your standards; in it all Lord, I know I am complete in You. You specialise in making the most amazing objects of beauty out of the broken and 'rejects'.

Lord, today I pray for all the people in similar states of total surrender all around the world that You will meet them at their point of their brokenness; that You will heal them spirit, soul, and body; mend their hearts and strengthen them in You. That the reality of Your Word which says "in You we live, move and have our being" will be our daily vocation like never before. That You will sustain us by Your eternal peace as we stay our minds on You. Amen.

Lord, may living our lives take on a special and new meaning each day. You give us a hope and a future. May the reality of Your presence overwhelm our hearts; and may we seek to feed on Your faithfulness and may remaining in Your presence be our daily desire. Amen.

The world may be in turmoil and all that we hear may be lack and pain, our hearts will remain steadfast seeking Your Word and resting on Your promises. As I seek You, You will cater for all that concerns me. Thank You Father, because I have the assurance that You are God and in You, all things hold together. Thank You for holding all in my life together even when I do not know where to go or what to do.

Thank You Father for all You do and for things You are yet to do in my life, in embracing necessary change in all aspects of my life. Amen.

Embracing change is about looking to God for strength to first believe in the identity He has made available to you. You have been adopted into the family of God and now have the rights of a son and you know who you are in God. Your identity can give you an idea of where you are at and where you should be heading to in your life.

Secondly, to stand - even in the face of huge opposition and ridicule from friends. Just aim to do and be the best that God has created you to be.

Thirdly, to keep going while striving for excellence and the best at all times.

Finally, to be humble enough to be sincere with yourself at all times. Do whatever it takes to be on the only path that God Himself has carved for you. Therefore, your instructions should be from above and above only.

I was moved by this write up on UCB daily devotional publication, word for today of the 21/08/2012 and I would like to end this book with it:

"...William Arthur Ward wrote: 'Believe while others are doubting. Plan while others are playing. Decide while others are delaying. Prepare while others are daydreaming. Work while others are wishing. Save while others are wasting. Listen while others are talking. Smile while others are frowning. Persist while others are quitting...' If you're always comparing yourself to everybody else, you'll never fulfil your potential. Paul talked about life being like a race, and how we should 'run in such a way as to get the prize.' Who are we competing against? Ourselves, really. Each person that's put his/her faith in Jesus can

receive the prize. That's good to know because there's always going to be someone faster, stronger and smarter than you. And when you feel like you can't go on, remember that God isn't just at your finishing line, He's running your race with you too - in many ways, your own personal trainer. Three important pointers for running your race of life:

1) Get going. Starting anything is often the toughest part, but do not be discouraged.

2) Push yourself. Our culture loves leisure time, but too much of it may mean you achieve nothing.

3) Do not give up. It is both how you start, and the way you finish that matters, so do not stop short when on to something good!

What now? All the gear but no idea? Read 1 Corinthians 9:25-27 then ask God what you might need to get rid of to make you more streamlined as you run your race…"

In closing, join me to meditate and memorize this scripture:

"Now may the God of peace [Who is the Author and the Giver of peace], Who brought again from among the dead our Lord Jesus, that great Shepherd of the sheep, by the blood [that sealed, ratified] the everlasting agreement (covenant, testament), strengthen (complete, perfect) and make you what you ought to be and equip you with everything good that you may carry out His will; [while He Himself] works in you and accomplishes that which is pleasing in His sight, through Jesus Christ (the Messiah); to Whom be the glory forever and ever (to the ages of the

ages). Amen (so be it)." – Hebrew 13:20-21 (AMPC)

It is your life, what you choose to do with it is yours and no one else's. Embrace change painlessly today by embracing God's Word!

Shalom.

References

1. Lukoff D, Lu FG, Turner R. Cultural considerations in the assessment and treatment of religious and spiritual problems. Psychiatric Clinic North Am. 1995; 18: pg. 467-485.

2. Gove PB, Merriam-Webster Editorial Staff. Webster's Third New International Dictionary of the English Language, Unabridged. Springfield, Mass: G & C Merriam Co; 1961.

3. Mayo Clinic Proc.2001; 76: 1225-1235. Religious Involvement; Spirituality & Medicine; Implications for Clinical Practice. Paul S. Mueller; MD. David J Plevak, MD; and Teresa .A Rimmers, MD

4. The Seven Habits of Highly Effective People by Steven R Covey.

5. Propst LR, Ostrom R, Watkins P, Dean T, Mashburn D. Comparative efficacy of religious and nonreligious cognitive-behavioral therapy for the treatment of clinical depression in religious individuals.

6. Koenig HG, McCullough ME, Larson DB. Handbook of Religion and Health. New York, NY: Oxford University Press; 2001.

7. Gartner J, Larson DB, Allen GD. Religious commitment and mental health: a review of the empirical literature. J Psychol Theology. 1991; 19:6-25.

8. Ellison, C.W. (1993) "Spiritual wellbeing: Conceptualization and Measurement". Journal of Psychology and Theology 11, 4.

About The Author

Dr Nona Joyce Edeki (NJ) is a Christian medical doctor and works as a Consultant Psychiatrist with The National Health Service (NHS), United Kingdom. Being a psychiatrist, she is no stranger to the workings of the human mind.

She is also a lay preacher with the United Reformed Church, United Kingdom.

NJ is passionate about teaching, sharing and communicating God's love contained in His WORD with others; trusting in the dynamic ability of God's word to bring about lasting change in every life situation.

She runs the MindWorkoutGym, an open CBT, Cognitive Behavioral therapy group in her local church, at events and conferences; where the word of God is engaged in a relevant way to influence thinking, emotions, behaviour, language use and choices. She also facilitates an hour-long early-morning prayer-group called KABASH PRAYER LINE - 365 days a year!

Even though she is already busy, she also has a presence with live sessions of the MWG BIBLE QUIZ CLUB on Facebook.

Dr Edeki loves to write and sing gospel music; she has served as worship leader in her local church. She is mother to three young men and lives with her three sons in Kent, UK.

Printed in Great Britain
by Amazon